"*The power of prayer has had a profound impact on my daily life. I believe that by making prayer a priority in your life, you can transform your days, months, and years. Kathryn and Nancy's stories are a strong testament to how praying over God's Word can help you, especially through the darkest of circumstances.*"
—STEVE GATENA, Founder and CEO, PRAY.com

"*In his timeless book of Proverbs, wise King Solomon penned these words: 'the pleasantness of a friend springs from their heartfelt advice' (27:9). Nancy and Kathryn's wonderful book puts skin on this proverb and reminds the reader of the healing power of authentic friendship. In the earliest days of the Christian movement, Jesus' followers established the practice of employing healing circles—putting those who had experienced the challenges, healings, and wounds of life as the primary caregivers for others facing their own difficult path. The healing offered by those who themselves had a similar season of trial in their own lives was seen to be more potent than almost any pastoral care the early Church could provide. Knowing Kathryn as I do and knowing Nancy as a friend and as her parish priest for over a decade, I have been fortunate to witness how their story—told with beauty, candor, compassion, and humor within these pages—has brought comfort and healing to untold numbers of God's children. I am grateful for their efforts and will turn to this book again and again as I seek to offer care to those I am charged to serve.*"
—THE REVEREND RUSSELL J. LEVENSON, JR., D.MIN., D.D. RECTOR, St. Martin's Episcopal Church, Houston, Texas, Author of *The Life and Faith of George H. W. and Barbara Bush*

TWO BY TWO

Conversations Between Friends
Navigating Breast Cancer

Nancy Bynon
Phil. 4:13

Kathryn
Tortorici
Matt. 18:20

NANCY BEDSOLE BYNON
KATHRYN LAVALLET TORTORICI

Favorite Recipes® Press

Cover Artist: Katie Garrison
Interior Artist: Barbara Lavallet

ISBN: 978-0-87197-615-4

Library of Congress Control
Number: 2023908408

Printed in China
10 9 8 7 6 5 4 3 2 1

 Favorite Recipes® Press

*Two by Two: Conversations
Between Friends Navigating Breast
Cancer* was edited, designed, and
manufactured by Favorite Recipes
Press in collaboration with Nancy
Bynon and Kathryn Tortorici.
Favorite Recipes Press works with
top chefs, food and appliance
manufacturers, restaurants and
resorts, health organizations,
Junior Leagues, and nonprofit
organizations to create award-
winning cookbooks and other food-
related products. Favorite Recipes
Press is an imprint of Southwestern
Publishing House, Inc., 2451 Atrium
Way, Nashville, Tennessee 37214.
Southwestern Publishing House
is a wholly owned subsidiary of
Southwestern Family of Companies,
Nashville, Tennessee.

Christopher G. Capen, President,
  Southwestern Publishing House
Sheila Thomas, President and
  Publisher, Favorite Recipes Press
Vicky Shea, Senior Art Director
Kristin Connelly, Managing Editor
Linda Brock, Editor

www.frpbooks.com |
  800-358-0560

Acknowledgments

We are grateful for our relationships with our husbands, our children, our family members, and our friends, who have supported, listened, and prayed with us.

Thank you to my husband, Sam, who gave me great counsel, wisdom, and encouragement during this journey. I cannot say enough thanks to my sons and their wives, Michael and Towns and Daniel and Molly, and my daughter, Gracie, for their patience and kind ears during this process. I also want to thank my sister, Margaret, who has been one of my greatest cheerleaders from day one and even more so today. As you know, I love each of you dearly.

—KATHRYN

Thank you to my husband, Steve, our daughter, Ashley, and our son, Conner. Many thanks to my mom and dad, Bruce and Carol, and my two brothers, Tommy and Stevie. Thank you to my friends and the medical team that helped me through this journey. I am forever grateful for your support and love. Love you to the moon and back. XO

—NANCY

Thanks to Sheila Thomas, our publisher, who answered a million questions over and over again, and to Linda Brock, our editor, who brought our story to life. Thank you also to Vicky Shea, who beautifully designed this book, and to Kristin Connelly, who kept us organized. The collaboration of these women tremendously helped us share our story.

Our relationship with God and you, the reader, was key to writing our story.

Foreword

"Two are better than one, because they have a good reward for their
toil. For if they fall, one will lift up his fellow."
—ECCLESIASTES 4:9–10

How true it is that friends are family members that we get to choose for ourselves. It is also a fact that friends make every event of life better. With friends along, our happy times are more joyful, our celebrations are more fun, our significant moments are more memorable. Even food tastes better when shared with a friend! In addition, the painful roadblocks that we hit in life are alleviated by the comforting presence of someone who really knows us, inside and out.

Nancy Bynon and Kathryn Tortorici were blessed to learn the undeniable importance of friendship during their sudden battles with breast cancer. Their story—the shock of diagnosis, the navigation of the medical world of cancer treatment, their learning to accept help and to depend on others— seems all too familiar until it is inserted into the context of their friendship. After all, what are the odds that two Christian girlfriends close to the same age, hailing from the same geographic area, graduating from the same university, belonging to the same organizations, and who shared so much of their lives together would end up with diagnoses so very similar within months of each other? And more importantly, what good could possibly come out of this seemingly bleak yet unique situation?

Nancy and Kathryn's eloquence and bravery in revealing their story is a gift not only to someone who may be facing a diagnosis of breast cancer but also to anyone enduring a life crisis, be it physical, emotional, or spiritual.

Through this book, these two friends link arms with all who may need some encouragement in their lives to let them know they aren't alone. And their perspectives are made even more poignant by this intimate, thoughtful, and sometimes painfully raw account of their journey together through breast cancer, a journey made lighter by the companionship of God and a good friend.

—Laura Levenson

Contents

Barbara Lavallet

Introduction

Going through breast cancer together revealed how important relationships are when fighting this unfortunate disease. Our desire is that this book will bring you encouragement, support, and hope if you or someone you know is dealing with cancer. Ecclesiastes 4:9–10 says, "Two are better than one, because they have a good reward for their labor. For if they fall, one will lift up his companion" (NKJV).

Let us introduce ourselves. We became close friends while we both lived in Birmingham, Alabama, through coediting a new cookbook for the Junior League of Birmingham. Over the years, we have remained close, supporting each other through graduations, weddings, funerals, grandchildren, and even when we both moved to different states.

Discovering we both had breast cancer at the same time—a road no one wants to travel—our friendship and our faith in the Lord carried us through the diagnoses, treatments, and beyond. Our relationships were key in helping us deal with breast cancer. Our relationships with each other, our families, and our friends were such a vital ingredient in overcoming cancer and being strong. Our relationships with God rerouted our fears and deepened our love and understanding of God's promises. Nancy was a nurse and is married to a doctor. Her approach to learning more about breast cancer was from a medical perspective, but she is the first to tell you she did not know much about breast cancer and had to do some research. Kathryn was a teacher before she had children. Finding new ways of understanding a difficult concept by relating it to something more easily grasped is one of her skills. Through the way the Lord has shaped our personalities and experiences, we have gained lessons in navigating tough events, like when you hear the words: "You have breast cancer."

Everyone knows someone or is related to someone or is that someone who has cancer. What we have learned and want to share will help that one, the family member of that one, or the friend of that one. Our focus is on relationships working together to conquer this disruption in life called cancer. Allow us to be your new friends—a new relationship—as we share our stories. We want to share what we experienced and learned to hopefully help you navigate this unwanted detour.

"You don't know what you don't know" has been a favorite saying that encourages us to be content with life's circumstances or encourages us to learn a particular endeavor. Before the diagnosis of breast cancer, knowing what to say or do when family members or friends experienced cancer was difficult. Knowing how to support, care, and, more importantly, love was simply a guess. Now, having worn the shoes and walked through this journey, we hope to give you a peek at the mindset a cancer patient may have. Let our experience allow you to gain knowledge about what you don't know.

Since recipes brought us together, we decided to share our love of cooking by adding a recipe at the end of each chapter of this book. If a recipe's title is "Fighting Cancer" and the doctors and cancer team are trained to be the chefs and sous chefs, they are the professionals. We are not doctors or chefs. We are homemakers, wives, mothers, and daughters, and we are passionate about cooking. Each item in a recipe is listed to clearly communicate how to prepare it even before the task of cooking begins. Measuring—knowing just the right amount—is also very important. When following a recipe, there usually is a secret ingredient that makes the recipe great. The secret ingredient we want to add as we make the recipe called "Fighting Cancer" is RELATIONSHIP. That item will be the key ingredient to bring about success, regardless of the expectation.

In this book, we share our experiences of navigating our way through our friendship, diagnosis, and treatment, and how we live today. In each chapter, Kathryn has identified Key Lessons from God's Word, revealing how the Bible is alive and applicable in our own circumstances. Any game you buy at the store has rules that, when read and followed, make the game more meaningful. The Bible is the same for us as we live our lives. Reading, studying, and following God's Word is living our lives how God intended. We have chosen a Key Scripture in each chapter that we feel is important to write down and maybe even memorize if you or a loved one is battling cancer. God cannot lie, and His Word is truth that we need to engrave on our hearts. We have developed and tested (and tested again) healthy recipes that are great for sharing with those with cancer or to add to your cooking repertoire. Finally, we have added pages for you to journal and track your days as you grow during a difficult time. Growth cannot occur without pain and sacrifice. Writing down prayers, answered prayers, and even unanswered prayers will allow you to see God's hand in your path. As you read each chapter, we pray that you will be encouraged and strengthened, that you will be brave, and that you will have endurance, perspective, and hope.

Our journey would have been incredibly difficult if it had not been for our relationship with each other and with our Heavenly Father. We invite you to accept our friendship as we share our hearts, the knowledge we have gained, tips to know, words to say, questions to ask, how to prepare, and how to measure as we walk with you going forward.

—Nancy Bedsole Bynon & Kathryn Lavallet Tortorici

Barbara Lassalle

CHAPTER 1

How We Met

Nancy: "Hey, KT! Are you packed and ready to head to Boston?"

Kathryn: "I hope so. I have been working on the talk I am giving at the meeting."

Nancy: "I know it will be a great talk, and we will have fun and learn a lot."

Kathryn: "I can't wait to share about the making of the *Tables of Content* cookbook."

Kathryn

Nancy and I have been friends for many years. We met each other while we were members of the Junior League of Birmingham, Alabama. The Junior League is a nonprofit women's organization that raises money and volunteers time to better the community for women and children in the city of Birmingham. I joined the group to be a part of an organization that betters the community. Meeting other women and gaining friendships are just a couple of benefits of joining such an organization. Never in my wildest dreams could I have imagined how much the league and my relationships would make me better.

> *"Find a group of people who challenge and inspire you,*
> *spend a lot of time with them, and it will change your life."*
> —AMY POEHLER

For nearly five years, I was part of a team that marketed and sold two of the Junior League's cookbooks: *Magic* and *Food for Thought*. Profits from the sale of these cookbooks, written by women in the league, contributed financially to the league. I love sales, marketing, and cooking. When it came time to produce a third cookbook for the league, I quickly raised my hand to join the team. Nancy, greatly gifted in leadership and her love of cooking, also raised her hand to help with the project. Together, we committed to work with a fabulous team of women to produce the league's third cookbook, *Tables of Content*.

> *"Never stop learning because life never stops teaching."*
> —KIRILL KORSHIKOV

The project took two years to compile recipes, test, test some more, and pull it all together. Nancy and I talked on the phone several times a day—every single day. Texting was not a common or easy practice during this time. We did not have iPhones like we do today. I learned to trust Nancy like a sister. Yes, we talked about our cookbook project, but we also talked about our lives, husbands, children, dogs, and everything else.

After *Tables of Content* had been published for several months, Nancy and I were invited to the National Junior League Convention in Boston. We were invited to speak on behalf of the publisher to tell the story of how we made the cookbook. It was a wonderful honor. Leagues from all over the United States were present.

Following our portion of the conference, we had the opportunity to sell our cookbook in the gift market area. I don't remember if we sold a lot of books or not because I received a phone call from my doctor in Birmingham that stopped me cold: "You have a spot on your breast—seen on your mammogram—that is highly concerning. We need to see you as soon as possible."

> *"Choose to care about the needs of others around you."*
> —RICK WARREN

It was all I could do to keep it together until it was time to leave for the airport. I was numb. I was having a nightmare yet was still awake. I was worthless to Nancy in making decisions. Nancy was the best friend I could have had. She took over! She called a taxi (no Ubers), checked our luggage (who does that anymore?), and got us on the airplane. We had to change planes in Philadelphia, which was a little chaotic. The airport was overflowing with people. I was practically paralyzed with worry. Sweet Nancy led the way. Due to construction at the airport, we had to take a bus to another terminal. We made it to the gate, but they had just closed the door to the plane. I am sure Nancy was exhausted from taking care of me and just wanted to get home, but her perseverance and determination got us on a later plane to Atlanta. We rented a car and drove through the night to Birmingham. During that long trip from Boston back to Birmingham, Nancy and I learned so much about each other. Our friendship grew enormously. I am so grateful that she took care of me.

The tests and a biopsy proved that the mammogram was a false alarm for breast cancer for me at that time. The drill of thinking "What if?" quickly faded away as fast as it came. I would not have the same test results the next time.

> *"A friend loves at all times, and a brother is born for a time of adversity."* —PROVERBS 17:17 (NIV)

> *"Again, truly I tell you that if two of you on earth agree about anything they ask for, it will be done for them by my Father in heaven. For where two or three gather in my name, there am I with them."* —MATTHEW 18:19–20 (NIV)

Nancy

What qualities do you look for in a friend? I look for loyalty, love, respect, kindness, honesty, and integrity. Kathryn has all of these qualities and more. I often laugh because Kathryn and I have a different story about how we met. I specifically remember being in the Junior League of Birmingham's workroom, printing something I needed for an upcoming meeting. I did not personally know Kathryn but knew who she was, so I said, "Rumor has it you are going to chair the new Junior League of Birmingham cookbook. I would love to work on the committee." I was thinking I would be involved by being a recipe tester. A recipe tester is someone who cooks a potential recipe and gives feedback about the success of the directions or the quality of the recipe. However, Kathryn asked if I would like to cochair the project with her. I jumped at the opportunity, and that was the start of a great friendship. Kathryn and I are so much alike in our passion for food, cooking, and serving others that this opportunity was right up my alley. I loved working by her side and with the many other women on our committee. In friendships, you can learn from each other. I have learned a lot from Kathryn. She is very creative and is a devout, positive Christian.

> *"A friend is one that knows you as you are, understands where you have been, accepts what you have become, and allows you to grow."*
> —AUTHOR UNKNOWN

As Kathryn mentioned above, we were in Boston to promote the newly published cookbook. Kathryn and I were honored to be talking about the Junior League of Birmingham's *Tables of Content*. After our presentation, we went back to the hotel room to relax. It was then that Kathryn received a phone call. The nurse on the other end of the line said that Kathryn needed to have a biopsy due to an irregularity seen on her mammogram, which she had prior to our trip. We quickly arranged to get to the airport and make our way back home. I was very concerned for Kathryn and knew that she had to be scared. Somehow, she rallied on, as we focused on making our way home as quickly as possible.

> *"Don't hesitate or talk about what you want to do. Just do it."*
> —GBENGA AKINNAGBE

Because the airport was under construction, we had to run to get to our gate. As we got closer, we realized that the normal route to the gate was blocked off, and we were directed to follow the detour. We went down some escalators in hopes of getting on a bus that would take us to our gate. Time was ticking as we waited for the bus. As we boarded, we asked the employee overseeing the people who were getting off the bus if we would make it to our gate in time to catch our flight. He assured us that we would. It wasn't long before we realized that we should have asked him to call and notify the flight crew that we were on our way. As we arrived at our gate, we were relieved to see that the plane was still there. However, because the flight crew had already closed the door, we were not allowed to get on board. Frustrated, we headed to the customer service counter and literally begged for a flight out. Luckily, we were able to fly to Atlanta, but unfortunately, we had to rent a car and drive to Birmingham, which was approximately 2 hours away. At this point, it was already midnight, and although we were both tired, Kathryn chose to drive the whole way home. My job was to keep Kathryn awake as she drove. I tried my best to keep talking but found myself having a hard time not nodding off. Together, we eventually arrived safely in Birmingham, and it was during this time that our sisterhood began!

Key Lesson

"The Amalekites came and attacked the Israelites at Rephidim. Moses said to Joshua, 'Choose some of our men and go out to fight the Amalekites. Tomorrow I will stand on top of the hill with the staff of God in my hands.' So Joshua fought the Amalekites as Moses had ordered, and Moses, Aaron and Hur went to the top of the hill. As long as Moses held up his hands, the Israelites were winning, but whenever he lowered his hands, the Amalekites were winning. When Moses' hands grew tired, they took a stone and put it under him and he sat on it. Aaron and Hur held his hands up—one on one side, one on the other—so that his hands remained steady till sunset. So Joshua overcame the Amalekite army with the sword." —EXODUS 17:8–13 (NIV)

In the book of Exodus, chapter 7, God told Moses that his brother, Aaron, would be his helper. In chapter 17, Aaron helped Moses in many ways, but when he helped Moses hold up his hands as he held the staff of God, it depicted how a friend can help you when you have little energy, which brings great comfort.

After I heard the news that I had a suspicious spot on my breast, I felt weary like Moses, but Nancy was there to hold me up and move me along. She never complained or left me. She kept me focused and protected me from fear.

Most people don't do anything for a friend who is facing cancer because they simply have no idea what to do. They are scared they may say something wrong. They are cautious, thinking that the friend may want to be alone during that time. Nancy did not know what to do but just DO. She took care of me by meeting my needs and helping me function. When it all boils down to it, that is what you should do when your friend or even an acquaintance is numb, hurting, struggling, and scared from hearing the possibility of a cancer diagnosis. Nancy was sensitive when I needed to simply be quiet, but she let me know I would not have to go on the journey by myself. Communicate that to your loved one or friend who is going through cancer. Relationships are key when you have cancer.

—KATHRYN

My grandmother was the perfect Southern lady, who was always ready with refreshments if friends stopped by for a visit. We lived two hours away, and our trips to see my grandmother were extremely special. I do not remember a time when she did not have roasted pecans for us as we waited for dinner. This method of roasting pecans was shared by her friend who claimed the pecans never burned when roasting them in a preheated oven that was then turned off. Pecans are perfect for snacking as well as sprinkling over salads or ice cream. —KATHRYN

PERFECTLY TOASTED PECANS

½	cup real butter
16	ounces raw pecan halves
1 to 2	teaspoons kosher salt

Preheat the oven to 425 degrees. Line a baking sheet with foil or parchment paper. Melt the butter in a large bowl. Add the pecans and stir to coat. Spread evenly on the prepared baking sheet and sprinkle with the salt. Place in the hot oven and turn the oven off. The pecans will roast while the oven cools down. Leave in the oven for about 1 hour or longer. Your house will begin to smell so good, and with this method, the pecans will never burn.

VARIATIONS

- Use various kinds of raw nuts.
- Instead of using ½ cup of butter, mix 3 tablespoons of pure maple syrup with ⅓ cup of butter.
- Sprinkle cinnamon on top of the nuts.

Key Takeaways

1. Friends rarely just fall into our lives; we must seek them out.
2. It is an honor and privilege to have a friend who will stop whatever they are doing to pray with you.
3. When a friend pops into your mind, reach out and let them know you are thinking of them.
4. Find ways to start simple conversations with others while you are out in public. Introduce yourself if you don't know them.
5. Always have room in your heart for more friends.

Our Prayer for You

Oh, Father, thank you for who you are and for giving us the opportunity to know you. Thank you for the gift of relationships with others who come alongside us in times of trouble and in times of joy. Help us be aware of others who need our support and love. Amen.

Your Key Notes

CHAPTER 2

Cancer Diagnosis

Kathryn: "Hey, sweet friend. How are you?"

Nancy: "I'm doing well. How are you doing?"

Kathryn: "I'm in Birmingham today
for my yearly mammogram."

Nancy: "I just scheduled mine yesterday.
Please call me after your mammogram."

Kathryn

My husband, Sam, and I had just moved to Atlanta, Georgia, for my husband's job. I had always said I would never live in Atlanta, but I knew in my heart this was the next chapter for us. The Lord had answered prayers for his company to grow, and thus, our feet were now in this amazing, busy city. After we returned to Atlanta from the Christmas holidays, the letter from my doctor's office in Birmingham was at the top of the stack of mail. Usually, a letter following my mammogram appointment was good news, saying everything was fine. However, this one held different information: "Please call our office immediately for an ultrasound test. The initial mammogram results show a suspicious area."

It was a very cold day in January when I headed to Birmingham and had the ultrasound procedure. Sam was by my side, giving me strength even though we truly hoped it would be another "everything is fine" result. Yet, this time the news to schedule a biopsy seemed more serious. Everything was not fine. More tests and a biopsy were necessary. Since we had just moved to Atlanta, we knew that finding a doctor in our new city was the direction we had to take.

> *"Nothing is more vital than prayer in Christian existence, and few things are more vulnerable to neglect."* —JOHN PIPER

We questioned our friends and neighbors, doing our due diligence to find the best doctor and hospital for us. Initially, I had had my medical reports and scans sent to one hospital, so I had to drive to that hospital, retrieve the reports, and hand deliver them to another hospital. I did not know Atlanta at all. I barely knew where the grocery store was located, which I now know was walking distance away. I used my GPS to learn my way around my new city.

My files and records were finally accepted by Emory, and appointments for a mammogram, an ultrasound, and even a biopsy were scheduled. I had to wait several weeks before they had an opening. The waiting was agony. Getting settled in my new house, painting, and decorating helped to get my mind off of the circumstances. Keeping busy during these days was comforting.

On the day of the appointment, my husband had an out-of-town meeting that could not be rescheduled. I did not have anyone to go with me to the appointment. I could have gone to the hospital on my own, but I was so grateful to have my husband's assistant, who drove to Atlanta just to be with me. I was nervous and scared. Having her drive, walk, and pray with me was so important. I am forever grateful for her relationship and kindness.

During the ultrasound, the technician found the spot they had found on the mammogram. It was small but was not supposed to be there. Immediately, the room was filled with doctors, nurses, and students from Emory—strangely all female—to see how a biopsy is done under the tool of an ultrasound. I love hosting parties, but never in my wildest dreams have I imagined a roomful of people coming to see me and my exposed breast. The doctor removed five little plugs from the area. They looked like baby goldfish in the bottom of the petri dish.

> *"The bad news is nothing lasts forever. The good news is nothing lasts forever."* —J. COLE

I would soon learn that I had lobular carcinoma in situ (LCIS) of the right breast. I was positive for estrogen and progesterone receptors and negative for HER2. I had no idea what that meant. Breast cancer was totally foreign to me and my family. I found myself on a road I did not want to be on.

Nevertheless, I learned what I needed to know about cancer. I also learned the value of friendships and that receiving love from others during this scary time is so important. It is key.

Nancy

When we moved to Houston, Texas, from Birmingham, Alabama, in 2011, my friends in Houston encouraged me to get into the well-check program at MD Anderson Cancer Center. Fortunately, I was able to get in, and I now go every year for my annual checkup. First, I have my mammogram, followed by seeing the nurse practitioner for a breast exam. Next, I see the dermatologist for a complete head-to-toe checkup.

In January 2019, I went for a routine mammogram, breast exam, and skin check. All exams went as I had expected. One week later, I received a letter that said they had found calcification in my right breast. So, what exactly does that mean? A lot of women have calcification in their breasts. Calcifications are small deposits of calcium and, according to my doctor, are not connected to the calcium in your diet. Calcifications can occur after menopause. I did not have it in my previous mammogram in 2018. I was told that it was something that needed to be further checked. I immediately called my nurse practitioner and was scheduled for a diagnostic mammogram. A suspicious spot was found, which required an ultrasound. During the ultrasound, it became clear that a biopsy was necessary. The technician performing the biopsy was thorough about explaining what was happening. However, it wasn't her words that I really heard. Instead, I heard the clicking sounds of the instruments removing the necessary tissue, which would determine my future.

Three days later, I was driving home when I received a phone call from the nurse practitioner. She was kind enough to let me get in the driveway before telling me that I had invasive ductal carcinoma in situ (DCIS) of the right breast. I was positive for estrogen and progesterone receptors and negative for HER2. Shock set in, and I felt like someone had just punched me in the stomach. There was no history of cancer in my family. How could this be happening?

When I found out I had cancer, I immediately blamed myself. I thought, "What did I do wrong? I eat well, exercise, and take my vitamins." When the shock wore off, I needed a plan.

> *"You have to be willing to give up the life you planned, and instead, greet the life that is waiting for you."* —JOSEPH CAMPBELL

My husband is a doctor, and he went into doctor mode. He made some phone calls to see what we needed to do next. We were assigned a team of health-care physicians at MD Anderson. I looked at this as a "bump in the road." I chose to believe that detours can make you go to your knees and make you stronger in your faith. I just had to get around or over the bump in the road with God, my family, and friends by my side.

> *"The great thing to remember is that, though our feelings come and go, God's love for us does not."* —C. S. LEWIS

It is hard not to try to guess the future. Try to focus on the here and now and get through one day at a time. When you feel scared, fearful, or depressed, know that nothing can separate you from God. He can make you stronger through your circumstances.

Key Scripture

ISAIAH 40:31 (NIV)

"*. . . but those who hope in the Lord will renew their strength. They will soar on wings like eagles; they will run and not grow weary, they will walk and not be faint.*"

Key Lesson

"*Consider it pure joy, my brothers and sisters, whenever you face trials of many kinds, because you know that the testing of your faith produces perseverance. Let perseverance finish its work so that you may be mature and complete, not lacking anything.*" —JAMES 1:2–4 (NIV)

In both the Old and New Testaments, the Bible tells us that we will have trials in this life. Hearing you need to have a spot biopsied for cancer is difficult. Hearing you have cancer is even more difficult. That news affects not just the patient but also friends and family. While the patient may feel like the only one in shock—experiencing fear of the unknown—the reality is by far the opposite. A circle of people is around you that is with you every step of the way: family, friends, other cancer survivors, the medical team, strangers, and most importantly, the God of the universe. Understanding the role of those relationships is the key to facing this storm. Knowing how and who to ask questions is just the beginning. Asking for help and prayers—being vulnerable—is not a weakness but a golden lasso. Focusing on a big God makes the waiting, the fear, the process, and the results easier to understand and grasp. A thankful heart will also cultivate peace and extinguish the negative thoughts.

"Then he got into the boat and his disciples followed him. Suddenly a furious storm came up on the lake, so that the waves swept over the boat. But Jesus was sleeping. The disciples went and woke him, saying, 'Lord, save us! We're going to drown!' "He replied, 'You of little faith, why are you so afraid?' Then he got up and rebuked the winds and the waves, and it was completely calm. The men were amazed and asked, 'What kind of man is this? Even the winds and the waves obey him!'" —MATTHEW 8:23–27 (NIV)

Picture yourself sitting on the beach. It is a fabulous day, and you are full of joy. Then, in the distance, dark clouds are quickly heading in your direction. The first thing that comes to your mind is: "Oh, no, not this!" Those clouds and the storm just disrupted your beautiful day. The longer you sit, the scarier the storm becomes. Taking action and seeking shelter gives you power to overcome those fears.

Jesus provides shelter from the reality of the storm of battling cancer. It is time to wake Him up in your life. Reading books (even this one), gaining knowledge, and talking to a lot of professional people will not give you peace from the storm like Jesus will give you. Take action! Make the decision to trust Him today as you face the unknown. The relationship you can have with God is only possible through what Jesus did on the cross. He paid the price for our sin by dying on that cross, so when we accept the free gift of salvation through trust and repentance, we can have a relationship with our Heavenly Father.

—KATHRYN

KEY RECIPE

This salad is a great way to consume vegetables and fruits each day. Make this recipe when you gather with friends and family for parties, holidays, cookouts, and beach trips. It is the perfect addition to every gathering.

GREEN SALAD

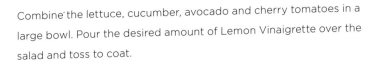

- 8 cups chopped lettuce (mix it up: kale, spinach, arugula, mixed greens, etc.)
- 1 medium English cucumber, sliced
- 1 avocado, cubed
  Cherry tomatoes, halved
  Lemon Vinaigrette (below)

Combine the lettuce, cucumber, avocado and cherry tomatoes in a large bowl. Pour the desired amount of Lemon Vinaigrette over the salad and toss to coat.

VARIATIONS

- Add pumpkins seeds, toasted pecans, sliced beets, cubed baked sweet potatoes or potatoes, diced apples, drained chickpeas, chopped boiled eggs, sliced strawberries, blueberries, corn, sliced radishes, or whatever fruit or veggies you like.
- Add a protein if desired.

LEMON VINAIGRETTE

2	cloves garlic, finely chopped
2	tablespoons fresh lemon juice
1	tablespoon maple syrup
½	teaspoon Dijon mustard
¼	cup apple cider vinegar
½	cup extra-virgin olive oil
½	teaspoon salt
½	teaspoon pepper

Combine the garlic, lemon juice, maple syrup, mustard, vinegar, olive oil, salt and pepper in a bowl and whisk to mix well.

Key Takeaways

1. Having someone with you at appointments to take notes, ask questions, and support you is helpful.
2. Never hesitate to seek another opinion if you feel uncomfortable about the plan of care.
3. Allow yourself time to comprehend your emotions. It is okay to cry, scream, and yell.
4. Identify your fear, write it down, and give it to Jesus.

Our Prayer for You

Dear Father God, thank you for your promise to always be with us and never forsake us. Thank You for being our shelter and protector. The relationship we can have with you is by far the most important relationship of our lives. We pray for those who are hurting and scared. Give them peace, comfort, and others to come along and help them during this stormy time.

"The grace of the Lord Jesus Christ be with your spirit. Amen."
—PHILIPPIANS 4:23 (NIV)

Your Key Notes

Barbara Lavallet

CHAPTER 3

Friends and Family

Kathryn: "Hey, Nancy. Just touching base. Call me when you have a minute."

Nancy: "Hey, KT. What's up? How are you doing?"

Kathryn: "Well, my emotions are leaking again."

Nancy: "This is going to happen and is normal. Do you want to talk about it?"

Kathryn: "Sam and I told our children today about my cancer diagnosis."

Nancy: "I know that had to be hard. How are you? How are they doing?"

Kathryn

Just as each person's cancer diagnosis is different than anyone else's, the relationships in each family are also unique. While families may be a lot alike, it is totally understandable that families do things, experience things, and communicate things in different ways.

Except for the time we surprised our children and took them to Disney World, I have a hard time keeping secrets from my children. My emotions are plastered all over my face as well as detectable in my voice. I chose to quickly communicate to my children that I had breast cancer. Sam and I called them on a conference call (before the time of Zoom), explaining the diagnosis and strategy, as well as the information we knew at that time. As expected, my children and their spouses all handled it differently. My oldest son asked a lot of questions, while my middle child gave me a lot of encouragement. The youngest, my daughter, was quiet with her emotions. The way my children handled the news of their mom being diagnosed with cancer is just a tiny reflection of how all our other relationships handle the news of a cancer diagnosis. It is fine to be inquisitive. It is fine to give encouragement. It is absolutely acceptable to just be quiet when you can't find the words to share. Everyone handles the situation differently. That is to be expected.

> *"Walking with a friend in the dark is better than walking alone in the light."* —HELEN KELLER

I chose to tell my children early after receiving the diagnosis because my children's faith in the Lord is strong. I coveted their prayers like one who is parched and needing water on a hot summer's day. Knowing we were praying together, corporately and individually, greatly calmed my fears and anxiety. I also told my sister and two sisters-in-law because I knew they would have my back by praying. My family was my little circle of prayer protection that I knew I could count on when I had days that made it difficult for me to pray. Their love, concern, and support through phone calls, text messages, books, and visits gave me strength. Being present was the best gift of comfort!

> *"You don't choose your family. They are God's gift to you,*
> *as you are to them."* —DESMOND TUTU

I learned so much from my children about how to respond to others who have a cancer diagnosis. Way too many times, I will just pray for my friend, which is the best thing we can do for each other. However, taking it a step further, I will send notes or food. Understanding the relationship between you and the other person is quite important. Knowing the person who is experiencing cancer, as well as their needs, helps to determine the best ways to support them. The best solution when helping others with cancer is to just do something. The worst solution is to not do anything at all because you assume that person is fine and has a lot of support. It is better to ere on the side of being loving with your friend or family member than to pass up the opportunity.

During this crazy time of emotions, you and your family members may not be able to define or communicate what your exact needs are. There were days when I just wanted to be quiet and not talk to anyone. If a phone call or text came in, I would make the decision to either acknowledge it at the time or return the call or message later. Knowing that I could decide what I needed in the moment (if I even knew), I felt a little bit of control over my situation. I was so grateful for the calls, messages, cards, hugs, and support. Those things weren't promised every day. It was special when someone reached out. I know how much it lifted me out of the pit of my self-pity, and I know I want to do that for others now.

Years ago, my mother was diagnosed with ALS, and she had a friend who was battling cancer. They had a third friend who would start a conference call with both of them each morning at 8:00 a.m. and faithfully pray over them. The time and commitment for this daily call was as much of a commitment as brushing their teeth; they just did it. However, the strength and encouragement for this group of friends was enormous. Not only did it affect the ones with the diseases, but their families were blessed by knowing others were loving and praying for their loved ones.

"Family is not about blood. It's about who is willing to hold your hand when you need it the most." —ARJUN SATHWARA

When I experienced cancer, my family experienced cancer as well. They joined me in prayer, strength, and endurance. Their friends lifted them up from their anxiety and fears. They needed support as much as I did. They also received encouragement when they knew I was being loved on by old and new relationships. Just like a little ketchup goes a long way, a little kindness goes a long way, reaching people you may never know. Relationships with your family and friends are key to fighting cancer.

Nancy

Communicating with your family and friends about your cancer diagnosis is something you never want to have to do. Imagine one of the most difficult tasks you will have in life, and this is one of those tasks. There is no easy way around it. There is not a right or wrong way. You will communicate the news to your loved ones in your own way.

"More information is always better than less. When people know the reason things are happening, even if it's bad news, they can adjust their expectations and react accordingly. Keeping people in the dark only serves to stir negative emotions." —SIMON SINEK

One of the reasons it is difficult to tell your friends and family you have been diagnosed with breast cancer is because a lot of people hear the word cancer and think of it as a death sentence. Nothing could be further from the truth. The first thing I wanted to assure my children was that cancer does not mean a death sentence. I was not going to die! At least not now. Only God knows the day, the minute, and even the second I will breathe my last breath. Since He knows that, I am at peace. Everyone will leave this earth eventually, but this was not my time. I wanted my loved ones to know that I was going to be fine and would be around for a long time. With the research and knowledge we have today, we have an array of options to choose from when fighting cancer.

"When you consider things like the stars, our affairs don't seem to matter very much, do they?" —VIRGINIA WOOLF

Just as every snowflake is different, everyone's emotional, physical, and spiritual reaction to the news of cancer is different. Some people are private and do not want to share the news right away. Others are transparent and do not hide the news from anyone. Your family and close friends are going to stay by your side through any kind of trials and tribulations you might be going through. The last thing anyone wants is for their family and friends to hear the news through the "grapevine."

I have discovered that people have a lot of questions, such as: What kind of cancer is it, and where is it? What stage is your cancer? How did you find your cancer? Are you having surgery? Are you having radiation and/or chemo? When is all this going to happen? These are all great questions.

I personally wanted to wait to tell people about my surgery, tests, and results until I had a clearer picture of my treatment plan. With any diagnosis, you have to make difficult decisions. Sometimes, it's not about the circumstances but how we are going to handle them. So, when I had a plan and knew what was going to happen and when, I would be ready for the "cat to be out of the bag."

> *"Do not be anxious about anything, but in everything by prayer and supplication with thanksgiving let your requests be made known to God."* —PHILIPPIANS 4:6 (ESV)

At MD Anderson in Houston, you are assigned a care team of people, who make decisions about your treatment. My team of doctors consisted of a breast surgeon and a medical oncologist. If you do not have to have chemo, a medical oncologist might prescribe a medication if the tumor is positive for estrogen. The oncologist will oversee your after-surgery care. If reconstruction of any type is needed, you may have a plastic surgeon. You may also need a radiation oncologist and a nutritionist.

Friends may feel helpless and may not know what to say or not to say. Sometimes, the best thing to do is to show up and just listen. One thing you can say is: "I am so sorry you are having to go through this, and I am here for you." We have so much to learn and understand from listening to someone else's story. It can be extremely encouraging and helpful to share experiences.

"If God has shown us bad times ahead, it's enough for me that He knows about them. That's why He sometimes shows us things, you know—to tell us that this too is in His hands."
—CORRIE TEN BOOM, *The Hiding Place*

A cancer diagnosis can make even a very strong person feel weak and extremely lost. The word "numb" would describe how I felt about everything. I declined many offers of help, but my friends knew I needed their love and support, so they would just show up or say, "I will be there on this date and time." Please share your thoughts and feelings and accept help when possible. Going through cancer is difficult. I truly enjoy journaling, which helps me be realistic and grasp my feelings.

"Therefore, since we have been justified through faith, we have peace with God through our Lord Jesus Christ, through whom we have gained access by faith into this grace in which we now stand. And we boast in the hope of the glory of God. Not only so, but we also glory in our sufferings, because we know that suffering produces perseverance; perseverance, character; and character, hope. And hope does not put us to shame, because God's love has been poured out into our hearts through the Holy Spirit, who has been given to us."
—ROMANS 5:1–5 (NIV)

"Draw near to God, and he will draw near to you . . ."
—JAMES 4:8 (ESV)

The whole cancer diagnosis process can be exhausting, and it is necessary to make time for yourself and breathe. When I catch myself breathing shallow breaths at different times of the day, I stop and take deep breaths. When I breathe in, I allow gratitude to flow in. Then, I let my breath out slowly through my mouth. Try to set a time every day to stop and rest. Take one day at a time. If that is all you can do, you have done well. Go outside and walk. Exercise and maintain a healthy lifestyle. It will help you to clear your mind and improve your energy. Most importantly, you are not alone. God knows exactly how you are feeling and has been waiting to reveal this chapter in your life. Celebrate the here and now. You deserve it, and life is a beautiful gift.

"If you do a good job for others, you heal yourself at the same time, because a dose of joy is a spiritual cure. It transcends all barriers."
—ED SULLIVAN

Key Scripture
PROVERBS 4:20–22 (NLT)
"Listen carefully to my words. Don't lose sight of them. Let them penetrate deep into your heart, for they bring life to those who find them, and healing to their whole body."

Key Lesson

It's fascinating how many times the Bible mentions the word "body." In the New Testament alone, the word "body" is found 144 times. The Bible talks about the human body, which in itself is quite amazing. Just thinking about the organization of how a body functions, thinks, reproduces, and breathes is mind-blowing. The body is a walking miracle.

Scripture also says that those who believe in Jesus are part of the body of Christ. *Adelphoi* is the Greek word Paul used in his letters when addressing the brethren of believers. With Christ as the head of the body, believers are the rest, with specific roles, purposes, and gifts.

"There are different kinds of gifts, but the same Spirit distributes them. There are different kinds of service, but the same Lord. There are different kinds of working, but in all of them and in everyone it is the same God at work." —1 CORINTHIANS 12:4–6 (NIV)

Later verses explain the purposes of the body and why different parts have different purposes.

"Just as a body, though one, has many parts, but all its many parts form one body, so it is with Christ. For we were all baptized by one Spirit so as to form one body—whether Jews or Gentiles, slave or free—and we were all given the one Spirit to drink. Even so the body is not made up of one part but of many.

"Now if the foot should say, 'Because I am not a hand, I do not belong to the body,' it would not for that reason stop being part of the body. And if the ear should say, 'Because I am not an eye, I do not

belong to the body,' it would not for that reason stop being part of the body. If the whole body were an eye, where would the sense of hearing be? If the whole body were an ear, where would the sense of smell be? But in fact God has placed the parts in the body, every one of them, just as he wanted them to be. If they were all one part, where would the body be? As it is, there are many parts, but one body.

"The eye cannot say to the hand, 'I don't need you!' And the head cannot say to the feet, 'I don't need you!' On the contrary, those parts of the body that seem to be weaker are indispensable, and the parts that we think are less honorable we treat with special honor. And the parts that are unpresentable are treated with special modesty, while our presentable parts need no special treatment. But God has put the body together, giving greater honor to the parts that lacked it, so that there should be no division in the body, but that its parts should have equal concern for each other. If one part suffers, every part suffers with it; if one part is honored, every part rejoices with it."

—1 CORINTHIANS 12:12–26 (NIV)

Everyone is different. We react and respond differently. We have different thoughts, fears, and ways of coping. When you have breast cancer, your children and spouse find their own ways of helping and encouraging. Allowing and accepting each behavior and knowing that God wired them gives us strength. The relationships with friends and each family member grows, and the bond between us becomes stronger. While those relationships grow stronger, we grow stronger in our faith and are grateful that God is always with us. These relationships—each with a different role and purpose—are the key to dealing with cancer.

—KATHRYN

KEY RECIPE

You can make this a simple cereal meal or add it to your favorite yogurt, and it's a great treat to share with friends. Place in a jar or clear bag, tie a ribbon around it, and give it as a gift.

HOMEMADE HEALTHY GRANOLA

- 2 cups extra-thick rolled oats
- 1 cup pecans, chopped
- 1 tablespoon whole flaxseeds
- 2 tablespoons cacao nibs
- ¾ teaspoon ground cinnamon
- ½ teaspoon sea salt
- ¼ cup coconut oil
- ⅓ cup maple syrup
- 1 teaspoon vanilla extract
- ¾ cup dried fruit, such as dried cherries or cranberries

Preheat the oven to 325 degrees. Line a baking sheet with parchment paper. Combine the oats, pecans, flaxseeds, cacao nibs, cinnamon and sea salt in a large bowl and mix well. Melt the coconut oil in a small saucepan over low heat. Remove from the heat. Add the maple syrup and vanilla extract and mix well. Pour over the oat mixture and stir until evenly coated. Spread evenly on the lined baking sheet. Bake for 20 or 25 minutes or until golden brown, stirring after 15 minutes. Let stand to cool completely. Remove to a bowl. Add the dried fruit and toss to mix. Store in an airtight glass container.

Key Takeaways

1. Reach out and call an old friend to see how they are doing.
2. Have lunch with a family member or friend. If they live out of town, have lunch with them over FaceTime.
3. A sweet friend shared with me the gift of "doodle journaling." Rather than writing in a journal, draw close to the Lord by drawing, painting, or gluing in a notebook relevant words or pictures cut out from old magazines.
4. Send a card to a loved one just because you can.

Our Prayer for You

Lord, we pray our hearts will be enlightened to see, hear,
and feel your love and power. Thank you for our families
and friends, our circles, and the hedge of protection around us.
We know we cannot do this without You or without them.
Please watch over us and guide us. Amen.

Your Key Notes

Barbara Lavallee

CHAPTER 4

Preparation

Nancy: "Hey, KT. It is time to prepare for surgery.
I chose to have a lumpectomy."

Kathryn: "That is what I am discussing with my doctor, too."

Nancy: "It is a same-day surgery if all goes well."

Kathryn: "I will pray for you and the doctors.
Take notes for me."

Kathryn

Cancer is a word we are all too familiar with, but how much do we really know? Sadly, hearing about a relative, friend, or old acquaintance having cancer is commonplace. My father had prostate cancer, and my grandmother had ovarian cancer, but I knew nothing of this cell-changing, life-threatening diagnosis. It was time to learn something new.

I love traveling! Planning a trip is one of my favorite things to do. I sit down and watch *YouTube*, go to *TripAdvisor*, read reviews, look at *Pinterest*, and research the best and most interesting attractions. I look up water-related activities, hiking trails, spas, and of course, great places to eat. Planning a trip is half the experience of the trip. To get the most impact from a trip, preparation is critical.

After being diagnosed with cancer, think of it as if you're planning for a trip. I used several reliable resources, like I do when I plan a trip. Using more than one resource is important. Cancer is not a "cookie cutter" problem, and neither is the solution. Breast cancer, or any other cancer for that matter, is like COVID-19 with its many different variants, symptoms, and ways to recover. Understanding the kind of cancer you have and how it is rated or what causes its growth is the beginning step toward learning how to prepare.

After my positive diagnosis with breast cancer, it was time to research. I studied the words around cancer: lobular, ductal, situ, and triple negative, to name a few. I read blogs and articles about the various forms and what they meant. Unfortunately, it was mind-blowing information, and I had a difficult time grasping it. I seemed to just mentally shut down.

My sister, a Certified Registered Nurse Anesthetist, came to my rescue as an advocate. The best way for my brain to understand the information was for my sister to do the research and then teach it to me. I also learned that knowing too much was daunting and scary and produced fearful thoughts. My sister would spoon-feed me information on a need-to-know basis. Her medical mind could grasp and sort the information about cancer and cancer treatments. It was amazing how she could discern relevant and irrelevant matters without even speaking to the surgeon or oncologist. On occasion, she had to shake me and raise her voice to make sure I was comprehending and learning what she was telling me. Her patience and determination in taking the time to educate herself and teach me is something for which I will be forever grateful.

"Most of the fragile insights that laid the foundation of a new vision emerged not when the whole group was together, and not when members worked alone, but when they collaborated and responded to one another in pairs." —MICHAEL P. FARRELL

Just like gaining knowledge from friends when planning to travel, I learned about cancer through my friends. A sweet friend of mine is a nurse oncologist, and I confided my diagnosis to her early on. Her questions helped me learn the language and terms that often look like a string of capital letters that have a special code or meaning. Drawing from personal relationships with people who are professionals or experienced with the same form of cancer is like having a friend tell you about the hidden gems of wonderful activities when traveling to a new place.

Newly living in Atlanta, I found it challenging to find a surgeon that I could trust. Where do you start? A dear Birmingham friend, who had moved to Atlanta years before we did, knew my situation. She was extremely kind and went above and beyond, researching information to help me find the right surgeon. Relationships with new and old friends can provide a wealth of information. The surgeon is one of the most important members of your cancer team. Researching, reviewing, and questioning is vital to finding the right person for you and your situation. When you put your life in someone's hands, it is a decision that is not taken lightly.

> *"If you have knowledge, let others light their candles at it."*
> —THOMAS FULLER

I finally understood what kind of cancer I had, as well as what kind Nancy had, when I pictured a flower. The stem is the duct. If cancer is found in this area, it is called ductal cancer. The petals, or flowers, are the lobular area, the milk-producing glands of the breast. My cancer was found in the lobular area. Both my cancer and Nancy's were in situ, which means they were contained, or found only in the place where they were first formed. Picturing a flower helped me understand my diagnosis.

When I was little, my grandmother used to tell me that I was a worry-wart. She thought I would dwell on my problems more than necessary. What she thought was a bad character trait, I used for good. My husband and I wanted to make sure we were receiving the best counsel from the surgeon. My husband's work friend had a connection to one of the country's top cancer surgeons from Sloan Kettering in New York. This doctor agreed to look at my file, and he confirmed the diagnosis and approved the direction of my treatment. Never hesitate to get a second opinion or confirmation. If you are uneasy about a plan of action proposed by the surgeon or doctor, pay attention to that feeling. The two words that echo in my ears are "Gain Knowledge." Learn and discern why you feel uneasy. I learned my surgeon respected me after I reached out to another doctor for confirmation of my plan and treatment. Ask your insurance company if they will pay for a second opinion. "Two minds are better than one" is a proverb that carries a lot of weight, especially when it comes to one's life.

Nancy

Confronting the decisions you need to make in preparation for your cancer journey takes an enormous amount of emotional energy. I often asked myself what I could have possibly done that may have caused my cancer. Like me, many find themselves wanting to place blame on either themselves or someone else. Eventually, I learned to focus on the fact that there is no future in the past. We can't control the future, but we have the present. Therefore, I decided it was best to focus on the here and now, learn from the past, and allow it to make me stronger. This process can be extremely overwhelming! I hope I can help you prepare. The Bible verse below is a great place to start.

> *"The name of the Lord is a strong tower; the righteous man runs into it and is safe."* —PROVERBS 18:10 (ESV)

From the moment I received the unexpected phone call from my nurse practitioner informing me that I had a small breast tumor, I knew that I had to prepare a plan of action. These are some of the steps that helped me:

1. When you go to your appointments, it is ideal to take a friend or family member with you. If this is inconvenient or if no one is available at that time, ask if you can FaceTime with someone. It is likely that your doctor will be providing you a lot of new information that can be difficult to process in that setting. It is always helpful to have two people hearing the doctor's plan.

2. As I had questions that came to mind, I would write them in the Notes app on my phone. Prior to my appointment, I would print the list of questions and take them with me.

3. I asked the individual who accompanied me to take notes as the doctor spoke. You can forget an amazing amount of information when you

are in a heightened state of stress. There will be a lot of information to remember and process, which can feel completely overwhelming! Recognize that this is very normal.

4. I would suggest gathering any test results that were performed at other facilities. For example, I had a suspicious mammogram at a hospital in a different state a few years prior to my diagnosis. I contacted that facility to obtain those test results. Also, collect any medical reports to take with you to your appointments because these can provide valuable information to your doctor. Document your medical history, like past surgeries or medications you are currently taking, and take them with you to your appointments. This will save you a lot of time.

5. This would be a good time to start a notebook to keep all of your notes and any information given to you. I still refer to mine, even after four years.

6. When fear and doubt set in, give it to God.

"Come to me, all you who are weary and burdened, and I will give you rest." —MATTHEW 11:28 (NIV)

As I mentioned earlier, I am a nurse. However, I had minimal knowledge about breast cancer. What I learned is that there are different types of breast cancer and staging of the tumor. This website is a great resource to review: https://www.healthline.com/health/breast-cancer/types-of-breast-cancer.

"Knowledge is love and light and vision." —HELEN KELLER

Key Scripture

PHILIPPIANS 4:19 (NIV)

"And my God will meet all your needs according to the riches of his glory in Christ Jesus."

Key Lesson

In the 1970s, my parents purchased the *Funk & Wagnalls New World Encyclopedia* for our family. These books could be purchased rather inexpensively at grocery stores and other markets. I loved it when a new book was added to the collection. Eventually, we had the entire set, complete with a dictionary, thesaurus, and years in review. These books came in handy when I had a research paper or other schoolwork that required research.

Learning and asking questions is a life skill. Having the right tools, like the encyclopedia, is essential to being ready and so is knowing where to turn when a situation arises. Be sure to use reliable resources.

When they had a question or a need in biblical days, they went to a prophet for answers.

"The wife of a man from the company of the prophets cried out to Elisha, 'Your servant my husband is dead, and you know that he revered the Lord. But now his creditor is coming to take my two boys as his slaves.' Elisha replied to her, 'How can I help you? Tell me, what do you have in your house?' 'Your servant has nothing there at all,' she said, 'except a small jar of olive oil.' Elisha said, 'Go around

and ask all your neighbors for empty jars. Don't ask for just a few. Then go inside and shut the door behind you and your sons. Pour oil into all the jars, and as each is filled, put it to one side.' She left him and shut the door behind her and her sons. They brought the jars to her and she kept pouring. When all the jars were full, she said to her son, 'Bring me another one.' But he replied, 'There is not a jar left.' Then the oil stopped flowing. She went and told the man of God, and he said, 'Go, sell the oil and pay your debts. You and your sons can live on what is left.'" —2 KINGS 4:1–7 (NIV)

This is the story of a woman who lost her husband and, yet, had a debt that needed to be paid. The people of the government were going to take her two sons and make them work as slaves to repay the debt. She was in a dire situation. What was she going to do? Elisha was a prophet, and the woman knew Elisha was the only one who could possibly help her. So, she found Elisha and asked him for help. Surely, his wisdom—the right tool—would tell her what to do.

I love how the lady expressed her need, her questions, her anxiety, and her anguish. Elisha was honest and trustworthy. The lady could not have done what Elisha told her to do without the relationship she had with her friends and neighbors. They came by her side and gave her vessels and jars. Their act of kindness did not help her entirely. The Lord who provided the abundance of flowing olive oil was the answer to her cry for help. The lady asked the question "What do I do?" She researched. She asked for help from Elisha. She did as she was instructed even though it may have seemed crazy, and the Lord heard her and met all of her needs.

—KATHRYN

KEY RECIPE

These tasty treats will soon be one of your favorite snacks. They are a great source of fiber. For an extra touch, drizzle with melted dark chocolate and sprinkle a tiny bit of sea salt on top of each ball. My granddaughter calls these "Nana's cookies." —Nancy

PEANUT BUTTER OATMEAL BALLS

- ½ cup crunchy peanut butter or almond butter
- ¼ cup honey
- 1 teaspoon vanilla extract
- ½ teaspoon ground cinnamon
- 1 cup rolled oats (preferably organic Bob's Red Mill gluten-free extra-thick oats)
- 2 tablespoons flaxseeds (optional)
- 2 tablespoons cacao nibs (optional)
- ½ cup chocolate chips (60% cacao chips)

Combine the peanut butter, honey, vanilla extract and cinnamon in a bowl and mix well. Add the oats, flaxseeds, cacao nibs and chocolate chips and stir to mix. Let stand at room temperature for 15 minutes to allow the oats to absorb the moisture from the wet ingredients. Shape into small balls, wetting hands occasionally to prevent sticking. Store in an airtight container in the refrigerator. Makes 15 to 20 balls.

Note: Cinnamon is known to reduce inflammation and help support blood sugar control. Cacao nibs are a great source of nutrients and a healthy fat/antioxidant.

Key Takeaways

1. If you have any questions or concerns, don't hesitate to ask. If you don't understand something, ask the doctor to repeat it and/or explain the statement.
2. Find an advocate who can help you decipher the language, meaning, and understanding of your situation.
3. We encourage you to read and gain knowledge about breast cancer.
4. Most hospitals and oncology groups' websites have links to support groups related to your cancer diagnosis.

Our Prayer for You

Dear Father in heaven, you are the creator of the universe and of all of us. You know all things. In faith, we ask you for the wisdom to comprehend this new path and direction. We pray for "straight paths" and discernment as we navigate this journey. Thank you for your loving kindness and comfort as we draw near to you.

Your Key Notes

CHAPTER 5

In the Waiting

Nancy: "Hey, KT. Just checking in.
What are you doing today?"

Kathryn: "Hey, Nancy! I'm waiting for
the refrigerator man to arrive."

Nancy: "So, you are just sitting there,
waiting for him to show up?"

Kathryn: "Well, actually, I'm doing a lot while
I'm waiting. I guess I should be thankful I have this
time to wait so I can get a lot accomplished."

Kathryn

Let's face it. Waiting is just part of life. Before we were born, our parents had to wait nine months before they could meet us face to face. Learning how to wait is an important skill in life and is even more important when you have been diagnosed with cancer. When I first learned about my malignancy, I wanted that lump to be out immediately. I wanted to be on the other side of the battle with cancer, even when I didn't understand what that looked like.

Back in the '70s, there was a television show called *Bewitched*. Samantha Stephens, played by Elizabeth Victoria Montgomery, was a nice witch, who could wiggle her nose or cross her arms and make anything happen. As a child, I loved that show and imagined what life would be like if I could do that. I could be dressed and ready in a twitch. Dinner would be prepared in a jiffy. The process it took for something to be completed would vanish. However, life is not like that at all. In fact, the process of waiting is practically the best part of the lesson of life. Waiting is quite necessary.

> *"To us, waiting is waiting. To God, waiting is working."*
> —LOUIE GIGLIO

My husband has said it many times in our marriage: "If you have to hurry and make a decision, chances are it will be the wrong choice." I found this to be true in my treatment of cancer. I had to wait after each step. Make an appointment; wait to be seen. Have a procedure; wait for the results. Make an appointment with the surgeon; wait for the meeting. After meeting with the surgeon—a vital step in the cancer journey—I had to wait for yet another appointment just to schedule an appointment to discuss the surgery. Between each step was literally about three weeks! It was very difficult to be patient but well worth the time.

While I'm positive the Lord was working on my heart and mindset and teaching me more about trusting in Him, I was at peace. Stand patiently as long as possible. He promises us that He hears our prayers. He knows what we ask even before we ask because He wants a relationship with us. Pray, believe, trust, expect, and wait on Him more than ever. Cling to the rope of hope through the power of God every single day.

"For there is nothing that God cannot do." —LUKE 1:37 (GNT)

Keeping busy—doing my job as a wife, mom, and friend—was my goal every day. Reading, learning, and understanding about cancer was my next goal.

"Hardships often prepare ordinary people for an extraordinary destiny." —C.S. LEWIS

Being new to cancer, I did not realize how many options were available to cancer patients. I will not be surprised by how many more options will be added to the list by the time these words are published in a book. Just the other day, I was watching a TED Talk of a surgeon who was in tears about the strategy used to handle breast cancer in the '70s. As soon as the patient was diagnosed with breast cancer, they performed a full mastectomy. He was so remorseful about this quick and horrible decision when it was probably so unnecessary. "Haste makes waste" is a saying we have heard all of our lives. What does that mean when you have cancer? I believe it means to learn the options, evaluate the risks, pray (of course), and decide on the best option for you. Every day is a step toward that choice and a day to overcome.

Nancy

"I waited patiently for the Lord; he turned to me and heard my cry."
—PSALM 40:1 (NIV)

Waiting can be torturous and can cause so much worry. Sometimes, worry can stop you in your tracks and paralyze you. We need to live one day at a time. A good friend of mine always says, "Left foot, right foot, breathe!" She also says, "Why open the umbrella before it rains?" Really think about that; most of the time we go to "what if."

So, why do we worry? It is the unknown of what is about to happen. Let this time bring you closer to God by relying on Him. Give your worries and fear to God as you wait for the next step. He is in control. When we worry about our problems, we miss the blessings of today.

"Do not let your hearts be troubled. You believe in God;
believe also in me." —JOHN 14:1 (NIV)

I tend to suppress a problem or deny it, which is not healthy. Acknowledging you have cancer can help you deal with it. Don't suppress your feelings and keep them locked inside. It will only hurt you. Talk about your thoughts and feelings with a friend or family member. It is scary, but you do not have to be alone. Make space for grieving.

"Therefore do not worry about tomorrow, for tomorrow will worry
about itself. Each day has enough trouble of its own."
—MATTHEW 6:34 (NIV)

I had my breast biopsy done on a Thursday, so I had to wait two or three business days plus the weekend to find out the results. Waiting for the results can be a very stressful time. I chose to stay busy. I love to bake; therefore, my neighbors got brownies and cookies that weekend.

Remember that your mindset can significantly impact your immune system. It can be easy to fall into "what if" thinking or get caught in the cycle of automatic negative thoughts. As Kathryn would say, "Don't go down that rabbit hole." We tend be in a hurry, and the world is passing us by so fast. We stay busy with busyness. We want our test results right away, but a lot of people ahead of us are waiting, too. The pathologist and lab team want to get it right. Sometimes, we have to wait for the insurance company to approve the surgery, doctors, and/or tests that need to be done.

Do your best to control your thoughts by focusing on the things that are going well. Incorporate self-care and do things that you love.

- Listen to music that will lift your spirits.
- Love more and laugh often.
- Take a break, sit, and pray as you breathe.
- Meet a friend for coffee or tea.
- If possible, get outside and walk fifteen minutes or do fifteen minutes of stretching.
- Journal and list things you are grateful for in your life.

Release the past and make room for new growth. Then, you will have room for miracles and new blessings. Be mindful and present in the moment, and let God be God and do His work.

Key Lesson

My family considers daffodils to be very special flowers. Every home I have ever lived in has had daffodils. Planting these yellow spring flowers was something I did to claim the house as our home. The history of the flower's meaning to my family goes back to my great-grandparents.

Highway 280 East has been my highway for a number of years now, because, you see, it is the road to my hometown, Opelika. Before the new by-pass, it literally ran by my house. If you follow 280 out of town on your way to Columbus, Georgia, you will pass another special place in my heart. It is our "plot of gold." Nestled right up against the highway is a pecan orchard that is part of the farm that my granddaddy, better known as Papa, bought over seventy years ago. He was the sheriff of Lee County and also raised cattle. The orchard was near the old farmhouse that once stood on the place, and that is where my grandmother Lois planted daffodils in the early days. As the years went by, she added several varieties of bulbs. I have heard she would get so mad at Papa when the cows would get in her orchard garden and trample her flowers. She died at the early age of 45, leaving Papa with a broken heart. In his grief, he decided he did not want to see the flowers that reminded him of her, so he turned the orchard back to pasture. He harrowed the whole orchard and turned in the cows. Grandmother Lois had sweet revenge, however. Those bulbs were divided and multiplied by the harrow and fertilized by the cows. The next spring, there was the most beautiful field of daffodils you ever saw. From then on, the field became hallowed ground, and once more, the orchard became a garden.

Through the years, my grandmother's bulbs have continued to multiply and bring joy to our family and friends. Every spring we all make a pilgrimage to the farm to gather our gold. We share the blooms with friends, make bouquets for the church and lavish our homes with huge baskets of the sweet-smelling flowers. The yellow blossoms have graced many of our tables at special family occasions. God has blessed our family with a precious treasure, and we are truly grateful.

—Barbara Melson Lavallet, January 30, 1999
(February 4, 1940–July 6, 2008)

Due to my husband's job, we moved to the city of Atlanta in 2018. The bank he worked with was merging with another bank, and it was decided to move the headquarters to Atlanta. We moved in faith before the closing, believing this was the next step for the bank and for our family. Yet, due to changes in the stock market and the plummeting value of the stock, which is uncontrollable, it did not make sense to go forward with the merger. What were we going to do? We had just packed up our house and moved to a new state. Should we move back? Should we put our new house back on the market? Should I just stay in my closet and cry? The one thing I knew to do was to do something. Get busy. So, I planted daffodils!

". . . for to wait is often harder than to work."
—PETER MARSHALL

I had ordered 250 bulbs to sprinkle in the front and back of the house. With every bulb I planted, I prayed. Bulb after bulb, I claimed God's promises. I gave thanks for God's faithfulness. I recalled past prayers, asking God to use our move to Atlanta for His glory and purpose. It was hard work and kept me busy. I don't think I'd ever planted nearly this number of bulbs in my entire life. I was planting new "seed" (bulbs) in a new "field" (city). I was mentally and physically exhausted when the last bulb was planted.

"The seed will grow well, the vine will yield its fruit, the ground will produce its crops, and the heavens will drop their dew. I will give all these things as an inheritance to the remnant of this people."
—ZECHARIAH 8:12 (NIV)

Lamenting means to express sorrow, disappointment, and grief. Job expressed his sorrow and grief after his family, home, and possessions had been ripped out of his life.

"At this, Job got up and tore his robe and shaved his head. Then he fell to the ground in worship and said: 'Naked I came from my mother's womb, and naked I will depart. The Lord gave and the Lord has taken away; may the name of the LORD be praised.'"
—JOB 1:20–21 (NIV)

Although my circumstances were not as painful as Job's, I cried to the Lord just the same. I gave Him my pain, my sorrow, the unknown. I trusted God was going to make something beautiful out of the situation.

"Mortals make elaborate plans, but God has the last word."
—PROVERBS 16:1 (MSG)

It was two days before Christmas 2018, and we were in Birmingham to celebrate my sister's birthday as well as Christmas with our family. Since I was in Birmingham, I scheduled my annual doctor's visit and mammogram. Afterward, I went home, settled under the covers, and took a little nap.

"Honey!!! Wake up!" Sam was hovering over me with the biggest smile. "The deal is going to close! We will close in a few weeks!"

The heavy burden was removed! I breathed a sigh of relief and was grateful for God's direction, faithfulness, and mercy!

When we arrived back in Atlanta after Christmas, there was a letter in the mailbox from the hospital in Birmingham. It was the letter that said I had something suspicious in my mammogram. They needed to do more tests. The "hurry up and wait" was beginning.

Transferring my records was challenging. I felt like time was precious, and yet, I could do nothing but wait. God teaches us so much during the waiting. He wants us to focus on Him and not our circumstances.

"But he said to me, 'My grace is sufficient for you, for my power is made perfect in weakness.' Therefore, I will boast all the more gladly about my weaknesses, so that Christ's power may rest on me."
—2 CORINTHIANS 12:9 (NIV)

"Therefore we do not lose heart. Though outwardly we are wasting away, yet inwardly we are being renewed day by day. For our light and momentary troubles are achieving for us an eternal glory that far outweighs them all. So we fix our eyes not on what is seen, but on what is unseen, since what is seen is temporary, but what is unseen is eternal." —2 CORINTHIANS 4:16–18 (NIV)

Four months after receiving the news that I had an abnormal mammogram, I was going into surgery to have a lumpectomy. It was so strange. I was having surgery at the same place my father had lifesaving surgery almost twenty years earlier. I never would have imagined this day. God knew it was coming, and He prepared me for it.

"What then are we to do about our problems? We must learn to live with them until such time as God delivers us from them . . . we must pray for grace to endure them without murmuring. Problems patiently endured will work for our spiritual perfecting. They harm us only when we resist them or endure them unwillingly."
—A. W. TOZER

God also prepared the surprise I would see when I came home from the hospital. The daffodils that I had planted months before, in a state of crying and pleading, were in full bloom outside every window of our house! Daffodils usually bloom in February, but it was April. God's timing is perfect! Our Heavenly Lord is so good! Flowers are like love letters from Him. He loves and cares for all of us and desires us to be close to Him.

"And we know that God causes all things to work together for good to those who love God, to those who are called according to His purpose. For those whom He foreknew, He also predestined to become conformed to the image of His Son, so that He would be the firstborn among many brethren; and these whom He predestined, He also called; and these whom He called, He also justified; and these whom He justified, He also glorified. What then shall we say to these things? If God is for us, who is against us? He who did not spare His own Son, but delivered Him over for us all, how will He not also with Him freely give us all things?" —ROMANS 8:28–32 (NASB)

—KATHRYN

KEY RECIPE

You can make this into an oatmeal steamer by adding your serving to a mug, adding milk of choice, and heating in the microwave to the desired temperature or on the stovetop in a small pot over medium heat. Then, add your toppings.

....

BREAKFAST BAKED OATMEAL

½	cup coconut oil, melted
½	cup maple syrup
2	large eggs, lightly beaten
1	cup milk (any kind)
1	teaspoon pure vanilla extract
3	cups old-fashioned oats
2	teaspoons baking powder
½	teaspoon salt
1½	teaspoons ground cinnamon
½	cup pecans, toasted and chopped (optional)

Preheat the oven to 350 degrees. Grease the bottom and sides of a 7x11-inch baking dish. Whisk the coconut oil, maple syrup, eggs, milk and vanilla extract in a medium bowl. Add the oats, baking powder, salt, cinnamon and pecans and stir to mix. Let stand for 15 to 20 minutes or until the oats have absorbed some of the liquid. Stir to mix well.

Spoon the oat mixture into the prepared baking dish. Bake for 30 to 35 minutes or until the edges are golden brown and the center is set. Store in an airtight glass container in the refrigerator for up to 4 days.

TOPPINGS (OPTIONAL)

Blueberries, diced apples or fruit of choice

Drizzle with honey or add dried cherries, chopped walnuts, cacao nibs, chocolate chips, or anything you like to add to your oatmeal.

Key Takeaways

1. If you are experiencing anxiety or fear, find a group of friends in your neighborhood or church, or see if your hospital has a support group that you can call.

2. Stay busy while you wait. Be productive rather than idle. Focus your mind on a project rather than fear of the unknown.

3. The process of waiting can be the most important and productive time.

Our Prayer for You

Oh, Father God, help us to remain faithful as we wait on You and what lies ahead for the future and the future of the family. Allow this trial to be the event that brings us to our knees as we put our lives in Your hands. You know what is best for us, and we put our hope in You. We give You thanks as we believe nothing happens outside of Your knowledge and will. Because of Jesus and in His name, we pray. Amen.

Your Key Notes

CHAPTER 6

Before and After Surgery

Nancy: "Hey, KT. Just checking in before I go to surgery in the morning."

Kathryn: "I'm so glad you called. I have had you on my heart."

Nancy: "While I should be a little nervous, I'm just ready for the next step."

Kathryn: "This is a big step, but please know you will be covered in prayer."

Nancy: "I am grateful to have you praying, and I thank you for your love, support, and friendship. Here we go!"

Nancy

As I mentioned earlier in the book, I am a nurse but did not know a lot about cancer, so I had to read, study, and learn. However, I do know about surgery. I worked in the operating room at the University of Alabama at Birmingham (UAB) Hospital. Being a patient is a completely different experience.

We can take every experience or situation and use it as a way to learn something new. I did not necessarily like being the patient, but I was learning a lot.

The day of my surgery happened to be Ash Wednesday (a holy day of prayer and fasting in many Western Christian denominations). The operating room was full of patients and their visitors (before COVID-19). My surgery was delayed because the pre-op beds were full of patients who'd had surgery the day before. The patients were being discharged or admitted to the hospital. We waited several hours for the pre-op rooms to become available.

After two and a half hours, I was called back to a room. My husband and son were able to go in with me. My daughter lives in Alabama, and since it was an outpatient procedure in Houston, I asked her to stay home. Several of my sweet friends waited in the waiting room until the surgery was over.

Surgery is a time when fear can set in if we let it—fear of the unknown, fear that something will go wrong, fear that the surgeon won't get it all, fear that something will happen to you, etc. All of the unknowns are a big source of stress, so try not to let fear deceive your heart. God did not give us a spirit of fear.

"For God hath not given us the spirit of fear; but of power, and of love, and of a sound mind." —2 TIMOTHY 1:7 (KJV)

Ups and downs happen throughout our lives. We cannot predict them or keep them from happening, but we can prepare for them and trust in God.

"Fear of the future makes people settle for things in the present that completely defy abundant life." —BETH MOORE

When preparing for surgery, wear something comfortable and easy to put on after the surgery, like a button-up shirt and pants that easily pull down and up. Slip-on shoes are helpful. It would be best not to wear a pullover shirt because it will be hard to raise your arms and pull your shirt over your head—a good excuse to get a new outfit to wear the morning of the surgery. As women, we love to look nice and feel comfortable.

Whether you have a lumpectomy or mastectomy is up to you and your medical team. As mentioned earlier, I chose to have a lumpectomy, which means to remove the cancer and any abnormal tissue. Some healthy tissue might be removed to make sure the surgeon gets all of the cancer. A lumpectomy should take about one to two hours, depending on the size and placement of your tumor. Your doctor may remove some lymph nodes under your arm or inside your upper arm and send them to the pathology lab to see if the cancer has spread. Your doctor might inject blue dye or a radioactive substance into your breast to help determine the lymph system flow to the nodes. The doctor will remove the nodes that the cancer could have spread to. After surgery, this area and incision can feel numb and sensitive. The incision was painful and numb for me. Since the surgery stretches nerves and can cause inflammation, the area may have a weird sensation and be sensitive to touch. It is important to keep the incision clean.

A week after my surgery, my husband and I were traveling to Alabama from Texas, which is a ten- to eleven-hour drive, to see our daughter, son-in-law, and granddaughter. I made it a point to get out of the car every couple of hours to walk around—something I highly recommend. As we were traveling, my breast surgeon called and said the pathologist was concerned that we might not have clear margins on one side of the tumor removal. She mentioned that we could go back in the same incision and remove more tissue to be sure, or I could have more radiation. I truly wanted to know they got all of the cancer cells out, so I decided to have a re-excision lumpectomy. The goal was to make sure they got clear margins and removed all the cancer cells. I wanted it done as soon as possible. Four days later, the surgeon went back in through the same incision. Fortunately, when they checked, they saw that they had gotten clear margins the first time.

After my surgery, a friend gave me a pillow that is shaped like a heart. This type of pillow fits perfectly under your armpit and can relieve pressure from the surgical incision. It also helps relieve shoulder tension. I would put it under my arm and place my seatbelt over it and drive with ease, knowing I had protection from any accidental bumps. It was great to take with me on the road trip to Alabama.

"'I will restore you to health and I will heal you of your wounds,'
declares the Lord." —JEREMIAH 30:17 (NASB)

Now, the surgery is over, and the relief of the unknown procedure is behind you. It is time to transition and start healing inside and out. It is important to take it easy and rest. I can't stress enough to simplify your life as much as possible. Look at your commitments and take a few off your schedule. It is time to say no to things that don't bring you joy. Whatever you do, do not give up or give in to the crisis situation. Sometimes, a crisis situation can make you sit back and reevaluate your life. It can improve you and help you grow deeper in your faith and in your understanding of how to make your life better, and it can make you stronger. Healing is hard work, and it takes time. It requires action, discipline, and, most of all, motivation.

"Do not worry about tomorrow; for tomorrow will worry about itself." —MATTHEW 6:34 (NIV)

Your doctor will give you exercises to do on the affected arm. It is important to do them so that you do not get a "frozen shoulder." Some exercises may need to be avoided until you heal. Be sure to ask questions. Don't stop moving. You want to avoided lymphedema, which is swelling of the soft tissues, caused by a buildup of lymph fluid. I asked for a lymphedema consult with the nurse. She had important information about the dos and don'ts after lymph node dissection. For example, you don't want to get needlesticks or your blood pressure taken on the arm from which you had your lymph nodes removed. It is important to avoid trauma and infection in that area. When traveling a long distance by plane, it is important to wear a lymphedema arm compression sleeve. I recommend a glove, too. The nurse will properly fit the sleeve and glove for you because you do not want too much or too little pressure. Don't hesitate to ask your doctor for a lymphedema consultation. My consultation truly relieved some of my worries about lymphedema.

Kathryn

Nancy's surgery occurred a month or more before mine, so she was able to share with me information about the process and the wisdom she had gained. This was so valuable to me. I learned so much from my dear friend. She prepared me by telling me what I should wear and not wear. She shared how she had organized her schedule, eliminating routine chores and meetings. She even shared how she prepared and froze dinners that would be easy to warm up for lunch or dinner. However, there are little aspects about surgery that are difficult to put into words. Since diagnoses, hospital protocols, and personal perspectives are different for everyone, learning from someone else's experience is just a reflection of what to expect.

> *"Never be afraid to trust an unknown future to a known God."*
> —CORRIE TEN BOOM

The day before my surgery, I had my pre-op appointment at the main campus of Emory University Hospital, where I had never been before. It was a different location from where I had my mammogram and ultrasound and from where I had met my surgeon. I spent almost an hour studying how to drive to the location, paying close attention to how long it would take me to get there.

Driving in Atlanta was one of my biggest fears when we moved to the city just a couple of months before this appointment. However, that fear turned into my greatest joy. Getting lost taught me how to take the back roads during rush-hour traffic. It taught me to identify neighborhoods that I found truly interesting. I discovered shops, markets, and restaurants that I would have never known about. With cancer, I felt a little lost. I did not know what was ahead. Yet, I learned more through the trial and am very grateful.

> *"Getting lost along your path is a part of finding the path you are meant to be on."* —ROBIN SHARMA

I arrived at the hospital for my pre-op appointment about two hours earlier than I was supposed to be there. I would rather be early than worry about being at the wrong place. The campus was quite impressive and intimidating. Buildings were everywhere. I parked in the valet parking deck and asked how to get to building C. I began my journey but got lost. After about thirty minutes of walking through halls and riding on elevators, I found the place where I had an appointment to give some blood samples.

Following that, I needed to go to the office where I would get my "markers." I would have an ultrasound to identify exactly where my little lump was located so the surgeons would know where to take it out. They would put little stickers on me and used a permanent marker to mark the exact place for my surgery the next morning.

I thought that I had plenty of time to arrive to this appointment on time. However, I got lost again; it is a big campus. There were many offices on the campus. I walked through a tunnel, along a skywalk, and down long hallways, and I rode on several escalators and elevators. My heart was pounding because my appointment time was quickly approaching. In a panic, I asked for directions. A kind security guard pointed to two big doors. I found the office just on the other side.

The office was full of people, unlike the wrong places I had found that had only a handful of people. The line to check in was long. I was sixth or seventh in line. As I looked around the room, I couldn't believe what I was seeing. I saw people without hair. I saw people without arms and people in wheelchairs because they did not have legs. I saw others with a suffocating crowd of family members around them and others with crying babies. Why was I here? I wanted to sit on the floor and have a full-blown hissy fit and cry, "Lord, why am I here? I don't want to be here!"

As quickly as I felt angry and discontent, I had a realization that I was doing all right. I had hair. I had both of my arms and legs. I did not have all of my family members surrounding me, and my babies are now grown-ups. I was very thankful for this realization. As soon as I signed in, I found a place to sit and introduced myself to the lady sitting next to me. I changed the channel off of me and onto her, loving and caring for her just by being there.

"Gratitude can change your attitude. Gratitude is your attitude. Gratitude now becomes your light of hope and a promise for a brighter day." —UNKNOWN

The pre-op appointment went well. They took images and marked where the cancer was located. They drew on me with permanent marker and placed little stickers pointing to where the surgeon should make the incision. I was ready for surgery the next morning.

Fearing I would never find my car to get home, I walked out the nearest exit, saw a valet, and handed him my card so he could retrieve my car. It was literally a few steps from my surgeon's office to my car, but I had been lost like the Israelites in the desert. I am so thankful I got lost because I learned my way around the hospital for future appointments, and I knew exactly where to go the next morning.

A few weeks before my surgery, I met my daughter in Starkville, Mississippi. She took me to her favorite boutique and candle store. She was very kind and insisted on buying me a comfortable outfit to wear to my surgery and during the days I would recuperate. We picked out some drawstring warm-up pants and a loose-fitting, sea-glass green cotton sweatshirt. Knowing that she was thinking of me brought me joy and peace. Surgery was a big deal, and feeling cute in my new outfit made me feel confident and prepared. I still wear that loungewear today and always think of her thoughtfulness and love. It also reminds me that God has a plan for me and that I shouldn't worry.

Key Scripture

JEREMIAH 29:11 (NIV)

"'For I know the plans I have for you,' declares the Lord, 'plans to prosper you and not to harm you, plans to give you hope and a future.'"

Key Lesson

When facing surgery, the patient has to have complete confidence that the surgical team will do their jobs as they were trained to do, be at their best and alert the day of the surgery, and keep all tools and surfaces sterile and clean. The patient is at the mercy of others. Trust is the only option.

I have had several surgeries in my lifetime, including three cesarean sections. Just like you might introduce yourself to the waiter or waitress in a restaurant to get wonderful service, introduce yourself to the team right before surgery. Make the situation feel a bit more personal as if those people were operating on one of their own family members. I have even prayed with my surgical team before. Getting to know their names and vice versa is the first step toward building trust.

I love the story in Genesis in which Abraham trusted the Lord even in the hardest situation.

"Some time later God tested Abraham. He said to him, 'Abraham!' 'Here I am," he replied. Then God said, 'Take your son, your only son, whom you love—Isaac—and go to the region of Moriah.

Sacrifice him there as a burnt offering on a mountain I will show you.'

"Early the next morning Abraham got up and loaded his donkey. He took with him two of his servants and his son Isaac. When he had cut enough wood for the burnt offering, he set out for the place God had told him about. On the third day Abraham looked up and saw the place in the distance. He said to his servants, 'Stay here with the donkey while I and the boy go over there. We will worship and then we will come back to you.'

"Abraham took the wood for the burnt offering and placed it on his son Isaac, and he himself carried the fire and the knife. As the two of them went on together, Isaac spoke up and said to his father Abraham, 'Father?'

"'Yes, my son?' Abraham replied.

"'The fire and wood are here,' Isaac said, 'but where is the lamb for the burnt offering?'

"Abraham answered, 'God himself will provide the lamb for the burnt offering, my son.' And the two of them went on together.

"When they reached the place God had told him about, Abraham built an altar there and arranged the wood on it. He bound his son Isaac and laid him on the altar, on top of the wood. Then he reached out his hand and took the knife to slay his son. But the angel of the Lord called out to him from heaven, 'Abraham! Abraham!'

"'Here I am,' he replied. 'Do not lay a hand on the boy,' he said. 'Do not do anything to him. Now I know that you fear God, because you have not withheld from me your son, your only son.'

"Abraham looked up and there in a thicket he saw a ram caught by its horns. He went over and took the ram and sacrificed it as a *burnt offering instead of his son. So Abraham called that place The Lord Will Provide. And to this day it is said, 'On the mountain of the Lord it will be provided.'*

"The angel of the Lord called to Abraham from heaven a second time and said, 'I swear by myself, declares the Lord, that because you have done this and have not withheld your son, your only son, I will surely bless you and make your descendants as numerous as the stars in the sky and as the sand on the seashore. Your descendants will take possession of the cities of their enemies, and through your offspring all nations on earth will be blessed, because you have obeyed me.'

"Then Abraham returned to his servants, and they set off together for Beersheba. And Abraham stayed in Beersheba."

—GENESIS 22:1–19 (NIV)

If you are familiar with this passage, you know that God was testing Abraham. God told Abraham to tie down his son and make him the sacrifice. However, right before he was going to give the killing wound, an angel of the Lord appeared and stopped him. Close by was the ram that God provided for the sacrifice instead. Did Abraham have enough faith in the Lord Almighty to obey Him even when it was the absolute last thing he could have imagined—sacrificing his own son? Abraham had such an intense relationship with the Lord that he believed and trusted Him completely.

According to many scholars, the ancient site of Moriah, the place where Abraham almost sacrificed his son, and Golgotha, the site where Jesus was crucified, may be the same place or in the same vicinity. I first heard this information in a sermon at church. I was blown away. God is so creative and threads everything together in perfect order and unity. Just as He provided a way for Abraham, He provided a way for all of us by offering the perfect sacrifice to pay for our sins through the death and resurrection of His Son, Jesus.

> *". . . but God shows his love for us in that while we were still sinners, Christ died for us."* —ROMANS 5:8 (ESV)

In my opinion, getting to know the surgical team by their first names is a step toward trusting that each person will do the best job. Although errors do happen, God does not make errors. Have you introduced yourself to God? How well do you know Him? Have you put your faith and trust in Him who is infallible and promises to be with you now and forever? Human beings are the only creatures that have a choice to follow Him. When we make that choice, our lives will be changed on this earth and eternally in the afterlife.

—KATHRYN

KEY RECIPE

A very easy and quick salmon recipe, especially helpful after a busy day. Salmon is a great source of protein and is high in omega-3 fatty acids.

BAKED SALMON

4	(5- to 6-ounce) salmon fillets
1	tablespoon olive oil
2	cloves garlic, finely chopped
2	tablespoons honey
2	tablespoons grainy Dijon mustard
1	teaspoon herbs de Provence (optional)
¼	teaspoon salt
¼	teaspoon pepper

Preheat the oven to 400 degrees. Grease a baking dish. Arrange the salmon fillets on a plate. Whisk the olive oil, garlic, honey, Dijon mustard, herbs de Provence, salt and pepper in a bowl. Spoon over the salmon fillets, coating the top and sides of each fillet. Arrange the salmon in the prepared baking dish. Bake for 10 to 12 minutes or until the salmon is opaque and flakes easily with a fork, broiling during the last 1 to 2 minutes if desired.

Key Takeaways

1. Wear loose-fitting clothes to surgery. You may prefer a blouse rather than a pullover top.
2. A spouse, family member, or close friend needs to drive you to and from surgery.
3. Be creative in meeting your surgical team. Write a quick letter to give to them or draw a happy face on your chest.
4. Change your perspective from "I'm going into surgery" to "I am going to have the best nap!"

Our Prayer for You

Oh, precious Father God, we are thankful that You know every hair on our heads and hold every tear we have cried. You know us inside and out. We thank You that You are infallible. You do not make mistakes. Help us to know You intimately so that our trust and confidence will be secure. Through Your Son, Jesus, who paid the price by His death on the cross, we can have a relationship that will never be broken. Amen.

Your Key Notes

CHAPTER 7

Receiving and Giving

Kathryn: "Hey, Nancy. I just got up from a nap. How are you?"

Nancy: "I'm better than I was yesterday. A friend brought us dinner. What a true blessing!"

Kathryn: "You need to rest. Your body is healing. My sweet friend brought us chicken potpie for dinner."

Nancy: "I am truly grateful for our family and friends. We could not do this without them."

Kathryn

Going to bed was all I could think about after my lumpectomy and the removal of three of my lymph nodes. I was still under the influence of the anesthesia and could barely keep my eyes open. As soon as I got home, I headed to bed, pulled the covers over me, and immediately fell sound asleep.

When I woke up, it was dark outside. The clock read 7:30 p.m. I could hear the sound of my husband's voice as he talked to someone on the phone about my surgery. With blurred thoughts, I remembered the day as if looking through a picture book.

I got up and went to our family room. Sam was sitting in his chair, enjoying something warm for dinner. A sweet vase of yellow roses was on the coffee table.

"Where did those come from? They are beautiful!"

"Someone from your Bible study dropped them off, as well as some chicken potpie from Lucy's."

Lucy's was a darling shop in Buckhead, Atlanta, that provided all kinds of gifts—food, flowers, and everything in between. I immediately felt loved!

> *"Love cures people—both the ones who give it and the*
> *ones who receive it."* —KARL MENNINGER

Being from the South, receiving kindnesses is sometimes just expected. However, if you just moved into a new town or city, the number of people you know is quite limited. At the time of my surgery, we had lived in the neighborhood for less than four months. I knew only a handful of people, who were from my hometown in Birmingham, friends from college, and those I had just met. I still felt like a visitor to this new community and city.

Getting to know others and forming relationships in a new city, town, or even on a new street is so necessary for many reasons. My precious neighbor from Birmingham told me something I will never forget. She said, "Whenever you are asked to do something with someone in your new community, go! If you have a conflict such as a repairman coming, reschedule the appointment. Meeting others is more important! Never miss an opportunity to meet new people."

Following her advice, I did exactly that. It did not take long for me to make some dear friends, who truly helped me during my time with breast cancer.

I had learned about and joined a neighborhood Bible study even before we'd bought a house in the neighborhood. My good friend from Birmingham had told me about it, and I knew it would be a great place to meet neighbors and fellow believers in Christ. It was one of the best decisions I made in my new community. The Bible study was open to anyone in the neighborhood, but a handful of committed women who had moved outside of the area still attended. It was a place where I felt encouraged, prayed for, and loved.

A friend of a friend of a friend invited me to go to a meeting of Christian women who were part of an organization that joins its resources to help Christian nonprofits. The group, known as One Hundred Shares, was started in Atlanta and is now located in cities throughout the United States. In this group, I met other Christian women who lived in my neighborhood. Some of these women were in the neighborhood Bible study.

I met one of my dearest new friends at this meeting. We began talking about our families and realized that not only did we both have sons but also that they both went to the University of Alabama, belonged to the same fraternity, and were in the same pledge class. We immediately became close friends. Every Wednesday, we would have "Wonderful Wednesday," when she would drive me around Atlanta to show me where to shop, get my nails done, or go out to eat. She was one of the special people the Lord put in my life to help me go through my cancer journey. Not only her prayers but also her presence and our relationship gave me joy and hope.

One day, I could not keep my tears from flowing. I was full of fear and disappointment and was just numb. It was Bible study day. I never missed an opportunity to meet other Christians, but there was no way I could find the energy or strength to go, even though it was one of my favorite things to do each week. I called my friend to tell her about my heavy heart. That afternoon, she and another friend came over to pray with me. I cried. They cried with me. It was the most special gift I received from those two dear friends.

May the God who gives endurance and encouragement give you the same attitude of mind toward each other that Christ Jesus had.
—ROMANS 15:5 (NIV)

Asking for or accepting help is not always easy. At times, you feel unworthy, or you think you can handle the adversity yourself. Once, when members of my Sunday School class volunteered to bring our family food after my father, mother-in law, and father-in-law passed away within a few months of each other, I felt quite strange receiving such kindness. I knew there were others who needed it more than we did. Everybody has difficult days, busy activities, and places to be. I felt like these special people did not need to be taking care of us. What I did not realize was that, by bringing us meals in our time of grief, they were loving and caring for our family like Christ loves and cares for the church. I also did not realize my emotions and energy were tied together; thus, I could barely think, much less think about what I would feed my family. Receiving the meals helped me and my family during that time of loss.

Receiving from others can come in many forms, such as texts, emails, notes, meals, gifts, and even a hug. My mother used to say, "Life is like that of a train. It takes two rails to get the train to its destination, the station, heaven. One rail represents joys and celebrations. The other rail represents trials and tribulations." Giving and receiving is part of those experiences. Relationships with others is what makes giving and receiving possible.

Nancy

Facing and fighting cancer can create some challenges so, now more than ever, rely on your family, friends, and medical team to help you navigate through your journey. The processes of receiving and giving have an important impact on relationships. Giving and receiving can be influential on you as well as others.

> *"The first rule of life is: Cherish your friends and family as if your life depended on it. Because it does."* —ANN RICHARDS

For me, giving is easier than receiving. Receiving is hard when you love to give. Trust me when I say that giving is the best gift. I love giving, and it brings me joy. I catch myself writing thank-you notes to people who are thanking me for something. Sometimes, we don't feel like we deserve a gift. It is true, but now, it is time for you to receive love and support and just say thank you. Try to accept it with gratitude. People may not know what to do or say. They are doing it out of love, and helping is an unselfish service. Your friends are concerned about you and want to do something. They are going through a difficult time, too, and you need to consider what they can do to help you or your family.

I was truly fortunate to have friends and family who helped me get to appointments and came over and sat with me. They would not take no for an answer. A friend of mine gave me fun socks to wear around the house. Another friend sends cards; that is her ministry and calling. A dear friend of mine picks flowers or greenery out of her yard and puts them, along with a sweet note, at my front door. I will get a text from her saying, "I was thinking of you and left a little something at your front door." That doesn't cost anything but can be so meaningful.

If you have a friend with cancer, watch for ways to serve, or simply ask, "How I can help, or what can I do?" One way to help is by being available physically and emotionally. You can run errands or just sit and listen. An act of kindness that doesn't cost anything can lift someone up.

Other meaningful ways to help: Send a text message, saying "I hope all is going well. Thinking of you." Send a joke or something that can make your friend laugh out loud. It will brighten their spirits. Pray and let them know they are in your thoughts and prayers. Ask what they would like to eat and drop off a meal. Drive them to an appointment and drop them off so they do not have to park in the parking deck. Go for a visit and watch a movie together. Listen, cancer can be a scary and lonely experience. Make a care package: a book, socks, a blanket, healthy snacks, bottled water, a hat, or a game or puzzle. Most of all, just be present.

"Jesus himself said: 'It is more blessed to give than to receive.'"
—ACTS 20:35 (NIV)

The smallest thing can be so meaningful to someone because it shows love. Love can transform those little things into big things in their heart. It can have a ripple effect, like throwing a rock in a lake causes the waves to ripple out.

Years ago, someone gave me this advice: "Give from the heart and follow your heart." So, give with compassion, and give thanks when receiving.

As we said in an earlier chapter, gratitude can change your attitude. When things are not going as planned, believe in miracles and receive them with open arms.

"Give, and it will be given to you . . ." —LUKE 6:38 (NIV)

Although we cannot avoid trials and tribulations in our lives, we can ask God for wisdom and ask our family and friends for support. Before I went into surgery, my friend/rector wrote a simple but meaningful prayer and texted it to me. I still have it after four years, and I truly appreciate it: "Dear Lord, wrap your loving arms around Nancy and comfort her during this uncertain time. Be with the doctors as they work to manage her care. And please provide strength as her body heals. In your name we pray, amen."

"Command them to do good, to be rich in good deeds, and to be generous and willing to share. In this way they will lay up treasure for themselves as a firm foundation for the coming age, so that they may take hold of the life that is truly life."
—1 TIMOTHY 6:18–19 (NIV)

Don't be apprehensive. Open your heart and receive love and support during this difficult time. You can learn so much. Jesus gave us the free gift of grace.

"Always show more kindness than seems necessary, because the person receiving it needs it more than you will ever know."
—COLIN POWELL

Key Scripture

LUKE 6:38 (NIV)

"Give, and it will be given to you. A good measure,
pressed down, shaken together and running over,
will be poured into your lap. For with the measure you use,
it will be measured to you."

Key Lesson

I am blessed with two wonderful daughters-in-law, Towns and Molly. God willing, Nancy will have a daughter-in law in His perfect time.

The book of Ruth is about the daughter-in-law of Naomi. Ruth stayed by Naomi's side even when Ruth's husband, brother-in-law, and father-in-law had all died. Ruth, also known as King David's great-grandmother, insisted on traveling with Naomi to the city of Bethlehem in a foreign land called Judah.

"But Ruth replied, 'Don't urge me to leave you or to turn back
from you. Where you go I will go, and where you stay I will stay.
Your people will be my people and your God my God.'"
—RUTH 1:16 (NIV)

Ruth gathered the leftover wheat from a nearby field that belonged to a man named Boaz. When Boaz saw her, he asked who she was. When he learned about her reputation of caring for her mother-in-law with such kindness, he fell in love with her and later married her.

"At this, she bowed down with her face to the ground. She asked him, 'Why have I found such favor in your eyes that you notice me—a foreigner?' Boaz replied, 'I've been told all about what you have done for your mother-in-law since the death of your husband—how you left your father and mother and your homeland and came to live with a people you did not know before. May the Lord repay you for what you have done. May you be richly rewarded by the Lord, the God of Israel, under whose wings you have come to take refuge.'"
—RUTH 2:10–12 (NIV)

This story is about giving, receiving, and love. The relationship between Naomi and Ruth demonstrates love that goes well beyond duty. The relationship between Ruth and Boaz illustrates redemption. Boaz buys back the family land from Naomi, marries Ruth, has a son, and keeps the lineage to David and eventually to Jesus alive.

Ruth's faith can be seen in her decision to stay with her mother-in-law even though she didn't know what was ahead. She did not know what her purpose was or what her future held. She had the faith to believe that God would provide for both her and Naomi.

"Now faith is confidence in what we hope for and assurance about what we do not see."—HEBREWS 11:1 (NIV)

—KATHRYN

KEY RECIPE

Roasting vegetables can be easy and simple. Roast any vegetables you have available. This is a quick 30-minute side dish to have along with rice, chicken, or fish.

OVEN-ROASTED VEGETABLES

20	small brussels sprouts, cut into halves
1	medium red bell pepper, cut into 1-inch pieces
1	medium yellow bell pepper, cut into 1-inch pieces
1	medium sweet potato, cut into ¾-inch pieces
5	carrots, cut into ¾-inch pieces
1	medium red onion, cut into 1-inch cubes
1	small head of broccoli, cut into florets
⅓	cup extra-virgin olive oil
2	tablespoons balsamic vinegar
1	teaspoon dried rosemary
1	teaspoon dried thyme
1	teaspoon dried oregano
2	cloves garlic, finely chopped
½	teaspoon salt
½	teaspoon black pepper

Preheat the oven to 400 degrees. Combine the brussels sprouts, red bell pepper, yellow bell pepper, sweet potato, carrots, onion and broccoli in a large bowl. Whisk the olive oil, balsamic vinegar, rosemary, thyme, oregano and garlic in a small bowl until well blended. Pour over the vegetables and toss to coat well. Spread the vegetables evenly in 2 baking pans. Sprinkle with the salt and pepper. Place the pans on the upper and middle racks of the oven. Roast for 25 to 35 minutes, stirring the vegetables and rotating and switching the pans after 15 minutes. Season with additional salt and pepper if desired.

Key Takeaways

1. Being there for someone and loving them is about giving, not receiving.
2. Find a way you can help someone physically or emotionally.
3. An act of kindness does not have to cost anything.

Our Prayer for You

Father, we receive so much from You, and we thank You for our innumerable blessings. Help us to share our love and blessings with others—our family, friends, and even strangers. Help us to receive with love and give with compassion through Jesus Christ our Lord. Amen.

Your Key Notes

Radiation and Chemotherapy

Nancy: "Hey, KT! When do you go for radiation today?"

Kathryn: "My appointment is at 1:30. I'm going early to make sure I know where I am supposed to be."

Nancy: "That is smart. Call me when you get home."

Kathryn: "You know I will. I'm ready for this next step to be over."

Kathryn

I'm not going to lie. I was nervous about the start of my radiation treatments. When you hear the word "cancer," you eventually hear the words "radiation" or "chemo" or both. Your oncotype score, the number the doctors give you after they send part of your tumor off to be categorized, reveals what type of therapy is required. My number was just under the amount that requires chemotherapy, so I just had radiation.

The fear and nervousness I felt having to undergo radiation was similar to riding Space Mountain at Disney World for the first time. This roller-coaster ride takes place in the dark, so the rider has no idea what is ahead. The unknown is quite scary. I recall being at Disney with my grandparents and standing in the long line to ride Space Mountain not long after the attraction first opened. I was shaking out of fear and just wanted to run from the line. Then, I vividly remember my grandfather telling me not to worry and that he would get on the roller coaster with me. We saw people getting off the ride, and they looked happy and thrilled, not terrified. If they survived with a smile, I was comforted to know that my grandfather and I would as well. Focusing on others who came through radiation is like watching those people getting off the roller coaster. If they could endure it, I could, too.

Emory Hospital had a campus about fifteen minutes away from my house. Going and coming from radiation would be extremely easy, even in the big city of Atlanta. I decided to make my appointments for the same time every day, except for Saturday and Sunday, for the next twenty-eight days. I chose 1:30 p.m. with the thought that I could be productive in the mornings with meetings or Bible study and head to the hospital after lunch. I read that radiation could make you tired. Going early in the afternoon would allow me a quick afternoon nap if I needed one. It was a great decision. I rested every afternoon, even if I just read a book.

I did have a few days that I had to be out of town and needed to miss radiation. When I had to be absent, I went in the day before at 7:15 a.m. for a treatment; then, I went back to the hospital at 4:45 p.m. for another treatment. The staff was so kind, and I was greatly appreciative of their understanding and flexibility. I'll never forget the mornings when I went to radiation at 7:15 a.m. The waiting area contained mostly men. I knew most of the faces—both men and women—in the waiting room when I went after lunch, but I did not know these men. An older man in a wheelchair had to repeat himself several times before I realized he was talking to me. He said, "Well, it looks like we have a new visitor to our class today." His words reminded me of when I was a little girl, visiting my grandmother's church in Opelika. The Sunday school teacher would say the exact same thing, and I would have to introduce myself. So, I introduced myself to the men and jokingly thanked them for allowing me to join their early-morning club meetings.

The waiting room becomes a short-term, or maybe long-term, place for the gathering of people with the same purpose. No one wants to be using the day for this activity, but you quickly realize that you are not alone. Everyone in that room who is receiving treatment has heard the same news you did: "Cancer." That room became a source of encouragement to me. These people became my new best friends, who understood my thoughts and emotions. I never even dreamed of this bond of unity but was totally grateful.

"Never regret a day in your life; good days give happiness, bad days give experience, worst days give lessons and best days give memories."
—LHACY MURRAY

Radiation is not as bad as I first thought it would be. I thought it was going to be like getting an MRI for thirty minutes every day, hearing that pinging noise going on and on. I learned to wear a camisole with a loose top to every visit, which made it easy to get undressed and dressed. I also learned to skip wearing jewelry such as necklaces. I could have skipped on the earrings, but my mother always taught me to never leave the house without lipstick and earrings. (I keep that rule to this day.)

The process of radiation is very similar to having a photo shoot except the room is dark, you lie on a table with various props the technicians set up, and you don't have to smile or even have your eyes open. I had little stickers, called markers, that told the technicians exactly where to shoot the radiation. Eventually, the places changed just a bit. Sometimes, they would use an actual permanent marker to draw lines. Because it was summer, I had to be careful to wear clothing that covered my chest. When the areas looked like sunburn, I put aloe vera on the spots. The technician also gave me Aquaphor, a healing ointment for cuts and burns. The radiation never really hurt until the last week. With all of the curling iron burns, hot stove burns, and an occasional sunburn I've experienced in my life, it did not bother me.

While radiation is not something I have to think about every day, I am still super careful about getting sun on my chest. I now wear a bathing suit that covers up my chest on the side my radiation was on. It looks like a one-shoulder top. When I wear other bathing suits, I usually throw on a sleeveless tank top to cover my chest. One time, I did not think the sun was very strong, and I did not wear anything over my radiation area. Bad mistake. When I came inside, it looked like a child had drawn all over my chest with a green highlighter. My radiation lines even showed through my white blouse! It did not take a long time for them to disappear—maybe a week or so—but it reminded me never to assume I was safe in the sun.

Although I only had to endure radiation, I know other cancer patients who have endured a more difficult journey. Having a friend or family member tag along to the appointments is an enormous way to feel loved and supported. The support you receive from having others by your side is a part of why relationships are highly necessary during cancer.

Nancy

Six weeks after my lumpectomy, I was ready and prepared for my twenty rounds of radiation. Kathryn had prepared me and told me what I needed to do. I had my outfit picked out and ready to go. My grandmother would always say, "You need a little color." So, like Kathryn, I don't leave home without lipstick and earrings.

When I went to see my oncologist just before starting my radiation treatments, she informed me that we needed to make a detour in my treatment plan. I was informed that I needed chemotherapy prior to the radiation. These daunting words were nothing short of immobilizing! I was told that the results of the genetic testing—used to determine the aggressiveness of my cancer—had been reviewed. The results indicated that my cancer had a higher risk of recurring; therefore, chemotherapy was recommended to reduce the risk of recurrence. This required four to six rounds of chemotherapy treatments. I felt frozen in time as tears trickled down my face. This didn't make sense to me. I kept saying, "Okay, stop. What did you say?" I truly felt lost in space, and I could not concentrate on what the doctor was telling me. After she had repeated herself three times, I requested to schedule an appointment for another time so that my husband could join me and help decipher what this meant and the best way to navigate this unforeseen journey. This is why we mentioned that it is so important to take someone with you or FaceTime with a friend while at an important doctor's appointment.

My body had shifted to survival mode since this was, in no way, what I had expected. I just wanted to get on with my life, yet the plans seemed to be shifting on me. All I could do at this point was to go home and make a list of questions so that I would be better prepared for the next appointment. As simple as this sounds, I had difficulty even thinking about what questions I should ask. This was all new to me, and my world was rocked. What now? My mind was racing and all I could do was pray that God had a plan much bigger than I could possibly understand.

When I met the oncologist again to further discuss my need for chemotherapy in addition to radiation, it was explained to me that the original treatment plan was based on the "early" knowledge of knowing the size of my breast lump and that the lymph nodes were negative. Also, the hormone markers (estrogen positive) indicated that the long-term survival rate was going to be great. However, results from the genetic testing indicated that, despite finding my cancer early, I was at greater risk of recurrent breast cancer! It appeared that my cancer would return if not treated appropriately. Having the chemotherapy in addition to the radiation could likely reduce the risk of recurrence. Since I did not want to be faced with recurrent metastatic breast cancer in the future, I chose to have the new treatment plan with the direction of my medical team.

The new plan my doctor proposed was to have six rounds of chemo, twenty rounds of radiation, and five years of taking an anti-estrogen pill (aromatase inhibitor). Needless to say, my mind was still racing, and I had a thousand more questions.

> *"We can ignore even pleasure. But pain insists upon being attended to. God whispers to us in our pleasures, speaks in our conscience, but shouts in our pains: it is his megaphone to rouse a deaf world."* —C.S. LEWIS

Chemo is not fun, and it is not for sissies. But I truly believe that no matter how painful our circumstances are, God will direct us for His purpose.

"If any of you lacks wisdom, you should ask God, who gives
generously to all without finding fault, and it will be given to you."
—JAMES 1:5 (NIV)

Although I am no expert, I would like to share some suggestions based on what I learned during chemotherapy. It is important to remember that your course of therapy may change as your clinical situation changes during the treatment period. Treatments may be added or put on hold as your body and the cancer react to the treatments. Everyone reacts differently, and you may experience something completely different from others.

1. When you go for chemotherapy, the medical team usually draws blood to check your "numbers" before each round of treatment. If your bloodwork numbers, especially your white blood cell count, is within normal range and you are cleared for chemotherapy, ask your medical oncologist to sign the orders for the pharmacist before you leave the office. This can save you time when you get to the chemotherapy center.

2. Ask your medical oncologist or the doctor in charge of your chemo treatments to write a prescription for an anti-anxiety medication to have available before each chemo treatment just in case you need it. For me, the first chemo treatment was the hardest. Once the nurse started the IV and a cold cap was placed on my head, I got very anxious and did not want to go through with the chemo treatment. My friend who was there with me suggested that they give me something to help calm my nerves. The nurse had to call the doctor to get an order, which delayed the treatment, and this heightened my anxiety even more. However, the

next time, I was prepared and so was the chemotherapy team. While I did not need the anti-anxiety drug every time, it was nice to have it on order just in case.

3. Chemotherapy causes injury to hair follicles, which can cause hair loss. The cold cap that I mentioned above is a scalp-cooling system that fits like a tight-fitting helmet or cap. The cold temperature reduces the blood flow to the scalp, reducing the amount of chemotherapy medicine that reaches the hair follicles. This will help many people—but not all— keep some or quite a bit of their hair during chemotherapy. The cap is extremely cold and can cause headaches. It can also be difficult to wear headphones or ear-pods when wearing the cap. Not every cancer center has this technology, and you have to pay extra for the cold cap treatments. (breastcancer.org)

4. I bought a small rolling suitcase to carry everything I thought I might need. It was easier to roll a suitcase than it would've been to carry a bag on my shoulder. These are the things I took for my chemo treatments: a throw-size electric blanket since it gets cool in the treatment room, especially if you are using a cold cap. To reduce the risk of neuropathy in my feet, I bought and wore "cold therapy" socks. Another good thing I took was a hot/cold neck wrap. (Someone at the chemo center would heat it in the microwave for me.) I would put it around my neck for warmth. I brought snacks and water. You may need to ask your treatment center if it's okay to drink and eat in the therapy center. Before, during, and after chemotherapy, it is very important to stay hydrated to protect your kidneys and reduce nausea. A book or magazines may be helpful to distract your thoughts. I truly did not feel like reading, but you may. If you like to listen to music, podcasts, books, etc., then headphones, earbuds, or a small speaker are good to

take. If you are wearing a cold cap, you can play your music on your phone or iPad.

5. I was encouraged not to get manicures or pedicures during chemo treatments. You want to avoid any possible way of getting an infection. It is important to wash your hands with soap and water often, especially before you eat. If you are not able to wash your hands, carry disinfecting wipes in your bag. Wearing a mask in public during the first week or so after each chemo treatment can help prevent you from contracting airborne infectious diseases.

6. Just before your chemotherapy starts, you may be given several medications, for example, anti-nausea drugs and steroids, which help reduce or prevent side effects from the chemotherapy medicines. My oncologist recommended taking an antihistamine (an allergy medication) before I went for each chemotherapy session. The anti-nausea medication might cause constipation, so drink a lot of water and eat a well-balanced diet. I lost my sense of taste during chemotherapy and had a weird taste in my mouth. Despite this, I craved sweets and pasta. The only things I could actually taste were sweets. It's important to eat as well as you can. Many oncology teams will have a dietitian you can speak to concerning your diet during treatment.

7. During my chemo treatments, I was given two different chemo drugs. Once, as I was getting the second drug, I started feeling funny and seeing "bubbles." My friend got the nurse, and she immediately stopped the chemotherapy and gave me more steroids and an antihistamine through my IV. All that to say, please let your nurse know if you are feeling unusual during your treatment. When I went to bed that night, I did not feel good. At about 4:00 a.m., I started running a high fever and became extremely ill. Lying in bed, I was trying to tell a friend where to

find the thermometer and the notes I had been given about what to do if you run a fever. Eventually, my friend was able to get me to the ER, where I was admitted for twenty-four hours to rule out an infection. It turned out that I had not gotten enough steroids prior to the treatment, which caused a severe reaction to the chemotherapy. Everything turned out okay, but I wish I had been better prepared, both for myself and my support team. So, I highly recommend keeping a thermometer handy and having your doctor's after-hours contact information easily accessible.

8. After each chemo treatment, you may be given a medication called G-CSF, which is a growth factor to stimulate your bone marrow to make white blood cells and platelets. This will hopefully reduce your risk of infection from the chemotherapy, which can temporarily decrease the effectiveness of your immune system. Usually, the medication can be administered via a patch or shot twenty-four hours after each chemo treatment. The first time I had the patch placed on the upper backside of my arm. It was very uncomfortable to sleep because I kept hitting the patch on the bed. The next five times I had it placed on my abdomen below my waistline, which seemed to work best for me.

9. Social support is very important. Ask for help and rely on your family and friends. It is hard to do this alone. I cannot begin to thank my friends and family enough for being there for me during my breast cancer journey and chemotherapy treatments. I was never alone, and they were truly angels sent by God.

*"Flowers are like friends; they bring color
to your world!"* —UNKNOWN

My daughter, Ashley, lives in Alabama; therefore, it was hard for her to be with me when I was going through chemotherapy. To make me feel better, she wrote encouraging sticky notes and placed them where she knew I would eventually see them. Some of the places she chose were the laundry room, in my Bible, in drawers I would open, by my computer, etc. I still have the notes today and read them often. This meant so much to me, and I would suggest doing the same for a family member or friend who is going through cancer or even a hard time.

When your plans are not going the way you thought they would, hold on tight to the promises of God, trusting and believing that there is eternal life.

*"'For I know the plans I have for you,' declares the Lord, 'plans
to prosper you and not to harm you, plans to give you hope and a
future.'"* —JEREMIAH 29:11 (NIV)

Key Scripture

JOHN 16:33 (NIV)

"I have told you these things, so that in me you may have peace. In this world you will have trouble. But take heart! I have overcome the world."

Key Lesson

I first learned about the three men in the Bible named Shadrach, Meshach, and Abednego when I was in the seventh grade. I was in a choir group at church that performed a musical about three men who were thrown into the fiery furnace because they refused to bow down and worship King Nebuchadnezzar's golden idol. The faith of these three men has challenged me to have the same faith and courage when life gets difficult.

> *"A herald then proclaimed in a loud voice: 'Attention, everyone! Every race, color, and creed, listen! When you hear the band strike up—all the trumpets and trombones, the tubas and baritones, the drums and cymbals—fall to your knees and worship the gold statue that King Nebuchadnezzar has set up. Anyone who does not kneel and worship shall be thrown immediately into a roaring furnace.'*
>
> *"The band started to play, a huge band equipped with all the musical instruments of Babylon, and everyone—every race, color, and creed—fell to their knees and worshiped the gold statue that King Nebuchadnezzar had set up.*

"Just then, some Babylonian fortunetellers stepped up and accused the Jews. They said to King Nebuchadnezzar, 'Long live the king! You gave strict orders, O king, that when the big band started playing, everyone had to fall to their knees and worship the gold statue, and whoever did not go to their knees and worship it had to be pitched into a roaring furnace. Well, there are some Jews here—Shadrach, Meshach, and Abednego—whom you have placed in high positions in the province of Babylon. These men are ignoring you, O king. They don't respect your gods and they won't worship the gold statue you set up.'

"Furious, King Nebuchadnezzar ordered Shadrach, Meshach, and Abednego to be brought in. When the men were brought in, Nebuchadnezzar asked, 'Is it true, Shadrach, Meshach, and Abednego, that you don't respect my gods and refuse to worship the gold statue that I have set up? I'm giving you a second chance—but from now on, when the big band strikes up you must go to your knees and worship the statue I have made. If you don't worship it, you will be pitched into a roaring furnace, no questions asked. Who is the god who can rescue you from my power?'

"Shadrach, Meshach, and Abednego answered King Nebuchadnezzar, 'Your threat means nothing to us. If you throw us in the fire, the God we serve can rescue us from your roaring furnace and anything else you might cook up, O king. But even if he doesn't, it wouldn't make a bit of difference, O king. We still wouldn't serve your gods or worship the gold statue you set up.'

"Nebuchadnezzar, his face purple with anger, cut off Shadrach, Meshach, and Abednego. He ordered the furnace fired up seven times hotter than usual. He ordered some strong men from the army to tie them up, hands and feet, and throw them into the roaring furnace.

Shadrach, Meshach, and Abednego, bound hand and foot, fully dressed from head to toe, were pitched into the roaring fire. Because the king was in such a hurry and the furnace was so hot, flames from the furnace killed the men who carried Shadrach, Meshach, and Abednego to it, while the fire raged around Shadrach, Meshach, and Abednego.

"Suddenly King Nebuchadnezzar jumped up in alarm and said, 'Didn't we throw three men, bound hand and foot, into the fire?'

"'That's right, O king,' they said.

"'But look!' he said. 'I see four men, walking around freely in the fire, completely unharmed! And the fourth man looks like a son of the gods!'

"Nebuchadnezzar went to the door of the roaring furnace and called in, 'Shadrach, Meshach, and Abednego, servants of the High God, come out here!'

"Shadrach, Meshach, and Abednego walked out of the fire.

"All the important people, the government leaders and king's counselors, gathered around to examine them and discovered that the fire hadn't so much as touched the three men—not a hair singed, not a scorch mark on their clothes, not even the smell of fire on them!

"Nebuchadnezzar said, 'Blessed be the God of Shadrach, Meshach, and Abednego! He sent his angel and rescued his servants who trusted in him! They ignored the king's orders and laid their bodies on the line rather than serve or worship any god but their own.

"'Therefore I issue this decree: Anyone anywhere, of any race, color, or creed, who says anything against the God of Shadrach, Meshach, and Abednego will be ripped to pieces, limb from limb, and their houses torn down. There has never been a god who can pull off a rescue like this.'

"Then the king promoted Shadrach, Meshach, and Abednego in the province of Babylon." —DANIEL 3:4–30 (MSG)

When facing cancer, followed by radiation or chemotherapy, you feel like you are coming under fire, like the three men from Jerusalem. These men were taken to Babylon against their will to be assimilated into the culture and become leaders. They displayed courage and faith in God even when it could cost them their lives. They chose to be thrown into the furnace, believing God could spare them if He chose to do that. They also believed that if God did not spare their lives, their deaths would proclaim their love and faith for their true Father God.

"Courage is grace under pressure." —ERNEST HEMINGWAY

Courage is the strength to endure, the will to keep going, and the mindset to overcome fear and pain. Cancer treatments require courage. Where does courage come from? It is a gift from God in the middle of the fire. Courage is achieved through relationships. Shadrach, Meshach, and Abednego had each other for support, and they also had the Lord in the furnace with them. When you face trials, unwanted situations, and moments of hopelessness, take courage. Gather your friends and cling to the Lord. These moments will sharpen your faith and prove your worth.

—KATHRYN

"These have come so that the proven genuineness of your faith—of greater worth than gold, which perishes even though refined by fire—may result in praise, glory and honor when Jesus Christ is revealed." —1 PETER 1:7 (NIV)

KEY RECIPE

This super-yummy smoothie requires little preparation and very few ingredients and is a great way to get in your spinach without tasting it. The fruits and spinach are a great source of fiber and vitamins.

SPINACH AND FRUIT SMOOTHIE

1	cup blueberries
1	cup strawberries
1	cup spinach
1	cup raspberries or blackberries
1 or 2	bananas (fresh or frozen)
½	avocado (optional)
1 to 2	cups coconut water or milk of choice (depending on desired thickness)

Process the blueberries and strawberries in a blender until smooth. Add the spinach and process until smooth. Add the raspberries, bananas and avocado. Add enough coconut water to make of the desired thickness and process until smooth.

Note: You may add peanut butter, yogurt, or protein powder. You may use many combination of fruits, including frozen mixed berries. You may add fresh mint, vanilla extract, cinnamon, Medjool dates (pits removed), or honey.

Key Takeaways

1. It is important to remember to be flexible because your course of therapy may change during your treatment period. It does not necessarily mean it is a bad thing.

2. After radiation and/or chemotherapy treatments, take time to listen to your body and rest.

3. Have courage, and God will direct your path. He is in control of today and tomorrow.

Our Prayer for You

Father God, we come before You to lift up those who are beginning the journey of cancer treatment. We know the anxiety they face due to the unknown path treatment takes them on. We pray for courage so that those who are struggling can face the day. Our Heavenly Father, help them to know that You will be by their side regardless of their situation. Please use the circumstances of this fiery trial to bring glory and honor to Your name and help their relationship with You be stronger than ever before. We pray in the powerful name of Jesus. Amen.

Your Key Notes

CHAPTER 9

Our Bracelet Mission

Kathryn: "I made ten bracelets last night."

Nancy: "I know you will make someone happy today."

Kathryn: "I have a radiation appointment at 1:30 and want to be fully 'armed.'"

Nancy: "I must have given away at least five bracelets yesterday at my appointment! I love giving them away; it brings me joy."

Nancy

I started making bracelets after watching my daughter create jewelry for her small business. She taught me how to make them and what patterns to use. I was amazed by how satisfying it was to make such beautiful pieces of jewelry. It was then that I started making bracelets as a hobby. I gave my creations to friends, family, and even people I had just met. I loved finding beads made from different materials, formulating the patterns, and stringing them, while watching television or while talking to friends on the phone.

Whenever my daughter, Kathryn, or other dear friends come to Houston, they love to go to the bead stores. There are rows and rows of beads to choose from. Beads come in so many colors, materials, designs, and sizes. When seeing such a massive collection, the first emotion is often to be overwhelmed. When my creative daughter would go into the bead warehouse, her eyes would light up, and she would say, "I'm in bead heaven!" She would start mentally working through our next designs. Just like with other things in life, it is hard to know where to begin!

My friend KT, who is also very creative, was equally giddy when she saw the massive warehouse rooms filled with beads, charms, and various types of string. She knew in her mind what she wanted to make. The wheels were turning in her head. You could see the excitement on her face. The weight of her bag from the number of beads probably caused the security guards at the airport to question what she was carrying when she traveled back home.

I would make bracelets for my doctors and nurses, the technicians, and the ladies waiting for their next treatment or appointment. It would make my day, and I hope it gave them something to help them remember me when we parted ways. I knew in my heart that I would probably never see them again. People in the MD Anderson waiting rooms were from all over the United States and world.

"What you are is God's gift to you; what you become is your gift to God." —HANS URS VON BALTHASAR

I remember the joy I felt the first time I gave away one of my bracelets. Seeing my friend's eyes light up when I rolled a bracelet off my wrist and onto her wrist was so delightful that I wanted to share that feeling even more. I was often encouraged to start a business like my daughter did, but it was the satisfaction of giving away the bracelets that fulfilled me. When the other person smiles after I roll a bracelet onto their wrist, it makes me smile. To me, the feeling is priceless.

I have learned that if I make a bracelet that I love to wear, I will eventually give it away. My favorite bracelet is made with different shades of blue, gray, and beige. I call it the beach bead bracelet (the colors remind me of the beach).

Kathryn likes to call it a "trickle effect." You do something, and someone else will want to do it, too. My neighbor came to me and asked me to take her and her daughters to the bead store and teach them how to make bracelets. Her daughters made hundreds of bracelets and gave them to hospitals in Houston, Texas, for the frontline workers during COVID-19.

Whatever act of kindness you do, I hope it brings you joy and lets the other person know that they are loved. Watch and listen for opportunities to serve. We can all make a difference with compassion and kindness. It doesn't have to cost anything but a little of your time.

"The King will reply, 'Truly I tell you, whatever you did for one of the least of these brothers and sisters of mine, you did for me.'"
—MATTHEW 25:40 (NIV)

Kathryn

In 2011, my sweet friend Nancy and her husband relocated to Houston. I was heartbroken. Knowing we could not meet for coffee when it was convenient made me feel so lonely. However, God turned my tears into shouts of joy when my husband became an executive of a Houston-based company, which meant I would get to travel with him to visit Nancy. Once, during a trip to Houston, Nancy picked me up from the hotel and rolled a bracelet made of beautiful beads onto my wrist. It was the sweetest gift. The gift bonded our relationship as friends even more than ever, no matter how many miles separated us. Her kindness was contagious. I started collecting beads and making bracelets to share with others.

I loved visiting Nancy in Houston. We always visited the bead warehouses together. One time, we went to this warehouse that was probably the size of five gymnasiums. Each room was filled with rows and rows of beads from the ceiling to the floor. I would get overwhelmed with trying to decide which beads I wanted, so I would pray in each room for the Holy Spirit to direct my eyes and heart to know exactly what kind of beads I needed to purchase. It was on that day at that bead place that blue jade became one of my favorite beads.

Just like Jesus sent His disciples out in groups of two to proclaim the gospel, a friend was given to me to experience the journey of breast cancer. My sweet friend who introduced me to the art, value, and technique of making bracelets was now my friend who would be traveling down the same path of battling this ugly opponent called breast cancer. Her love, questions, and wisdom were a huge part of the peace that God, in His mercy, provided for me during this unwanted time. Together but miles apart, we encouraged each other during our illnesses and continued to make bracelets. Two of my favorite quotes that we repeated to each other during our many trips to the doctors' offices and cancer treatments were: "Are you armed?" or "How many bracelets did you give away today?"

> *"And do not forget to do good and to share with others, for with such sacrifices God is pleased."* —HEBREWS 13:16 (NIV)

On the mornings of my radiation treatments, I would put on two, three, or sometimes four bracelets while getting dressed. I would wear a bracelet made with blue jade beads with either a silver or gold square cross bead. I was so excited about giving away my little beaded treasures that receiving radiation treatments was an afterthought. I loved meeting others on the same journey that I was taking. I would roll a blue jade beaded bracelet off my wrist and roll it onto the wrist of a fellow cancer patient undergoing radiation treatment. I explained that the blue bead reminded me of the vast blue sky, which makes me feel like I am in the presence of God. I would point out the square cross from Israel and share that only through the death and resurrection of Jesus can we be in the presence of the Lord now and for all eternity. I would then tell them that this free gift of salvation was theirs to accept, just like receiving the gift of the bracelet.

> *"The right word at the right time is like a custom-made piece of jewelry."* —PROVERBS 25:11 (MSG)

My new friends in the radiation waiting room and I bonded. Tears of emotion were shared most days. I gave bracelets to all kinds of people: wives, grandmothers, mothers, granddaughters, hospital personnel, doctors, nurses, and new friends. Giving something to someone makes it personal. When you are personal, sharing your heart with others flows naturally.

During the first several weeks that I went to radiation, I noticed a small-framed man sitting in the same chair every day. He was quiet and never talked to anyone. I realized that he watched and listened to every conversation I had in that waiting room. I knew he did not want a bracelet, but what could I give to him instead? Having recently moved to Georgia, I learned that pecans are just as important in Georgia as peaches. The next day, I brought this little man a bag of roasted pecans tied with a blue ribbon. I walked up and introduced myself and offered an apology.

"Hello! I must apologize to you. I have not introduced myself yet. I am Kathryn Tortorici, a fellow patient receiving radiation today. Since I did not think you would like a beaded bracelet, I made you some roasted pecans the way my grandmother taught me to roast them."

He looked me square in the eye and said, "Thank you so much, but I can't eat pecans."

With that, I smiled and said, "No worries! I get to bring you a surprise tomorrow because I am sure we will see each other then!" That was the beginning of my friendship with Bruce.

"God gives us things to share; God doesn't give us things to hold."
—MOTHER TERESA

The next day, I brought my new friend a bag of Peppermint Patties tied with another blue ribbon. I shared with him about the significance of the color blue—how it reminded me of the vast blue sky and of being in God's presence. From that day forward, Bruce and I talked every time we saw each other. On the last day of radiation, I walked out into the waiting room. I did not see Bruce sitting in the same old chair. Bruce was walking up to everyone saying, "Hi, John. Hey, Bill! How are you, Barbara?" It melted my heart to see the man who had been so quiet become so radiant with joy, meeting and engaging with everyone. Only God could reveal Himself to Bruce, opening his eyes to see that having a relationship with the Lord and with others is the most important lesson for all of us. I praise the Lord for the opportunity to share bracelets, Peppermint Patties, and God's love and to see how that was spreading to others. What a blessing!

Key Scripture

COLOSSIANS 2:2–3 (NIV)

My goal is that they may be encouraged in heart and united in love, so that they may have the full riches of complete understanding, in order that they may know the mystery of God, namely, Christ, in whom are hidden all the treasures of wisdom and knowledge.

Key Lesson

When my husband was on his very first Zoom call after the pandemic hit, I was curious what this new way of communication was and was peering over his shoulder. Then, I found myself more curious about the books that were on the bookshelf next to his chair. I had no idea what was on the shelves that I had organized just a few months earlier. I noticed a cute little golden book called *My Dream of Heaven*. I took it off the shelf and enjoyed every minute while reading the book that was written in 1898 and republished in 2004. Reading a chapter before bed was like enjoying the best piece of chocolate ever made. A few weeks later, the COVID-19 pandemic shut down everything. With the extra time, I finally unpacked a few boxes that were still in the basement. In one of those boxes, I found my parents' book *Heaven* by Randy Alcorn. I began reading that, too.

For two years, I had planned a wonderful trip to Alaska for my family. My desire was to show them a glimpse of heaven. When you are in Alaska, your senses are heightened—they feel so alive. Everything is crisp and clean. However, the pandemic caused us to cancel that trip because Alaska had closed its borders. Since we all had that time reserved for a vacation, we rented a house on the beach and enjoyed that instead of the trip to Alaska.

A few days before we were to leave, a co-worker of my husband's sent him a book called *Imagine Heaven* by John Bourke. I grabbed the book and asked my husband if I could read it first. Sitting on the beach or by the pool, I would read parts of the book to my family. "Oh, listen to what this girl who had been deaf her whole life heard when she went to heaven. . ." or "You are not going to believe the sights this blind man saw when he went to heaven." While our family did not get to experience Alaska, our sweet Lord gave me my heart's desire to give a glimpse of heaven to my children. His ways are higher than our ways.

When cleaning out the attic of our mountain cabin a few weeks later, I found a children's book called *Heaven Has a Floor* by Evelyn Roberts. All of these books, as well the book of Revelation, have given me a clear visual of what to expect when I get to heaven. I particularly like learning about the incredible wall that will be around the grand new city of Jerusalem.

"The foundations of the city walls were decorated with every kind of precious stone. The first foundation was jasper, the second sapphire, the third agate, the fourth emerald, the fifth onyx, the sixth ruby, the seventh chrysolite, the eighth beryl, the ninth topaz, the tenth turquoise, the eleventh jacinth, and the twelfth amethyst. The twelve gates were twelve pearls, each gate made of a single pearl.
The great street of the city was of gold, as pure as transparent glass."
—REVELATION 21:19–21 (NIV)

Beads can be made with many different materials, such as wood, bone, metals, plastic, glass, and natural stones, like the ones mentioned in the book of Revelation. Natural stones are some of my favorite beads. Stones are made by our Heavenly Father, the Creator of all things. He used such precious stones in the wall around the new city. Many people are misled and worship the creation—the stone itself—claiming that certain stones have power. Only our Lord has the power to heal and give joy and peace.

—KATHRYN

KEY RECIPE

Eating vegetables every day is so important. A nutritionist told Nancy that it is important to eat at least two handfuls of spinach every day. It has so many health benefits. This recipe is a good way to get in your vegetables for the day and feel satisfied.

SPINACH FARRO SALAD BOWL

½	cup farro
	Vegetable broth
2	cups baby spinach
¼	cup brussels sprouts, cooked and sliced
¼	cup chopped tomatoes
½	medium avocado, diced or sliced
2	tablespoons toasted raw nuts, such as walnuts, almonds or pecans
¼	cup rinsed and drained chickpeas
¼	cup seeded and diced cucumber
	Lemon Maple Vinaigrette to taste (at right)

Cook the farro in vegetable broth according to the package directions; drain. Place the spinach in a bowl. Add the warm farro; it will wilt the spinach. Add the brussels sprouts, tomatoes, avocado, nuts, chickpeas and cucumber. Drizzle with Lemon Maple Vinaigrette and toss to mix.

Note: You may substitute another protein, such as chicken or fish, for the chickpeas and/or substitute another grain, such as rice or quinoa, for the farro.

LEMON MAPLE VINAIGRETTE

- ½ cup extra-virgin olive oil
- ¼ cup apple cider vinegar or red wine vinegar
- ½ tablespoon maple syrup
- 2 teaspoons fresh lemon juice
- 1 teaspoon Dijon mustard
- 2 cloves garlic, finely chopped

  Salt and pepper to taste

Combine the olive oil, vinegar, maple syrup, lemon juice, Dijon mustard, garlic, salt and pepper in a bowl and whisk to blend well. Store in a glass jar with a tight-fitting lid.

Key Takeaways

1. The greatest gift of life is relationship.
2. Don't forget that the nurses, doctors, office staff, and specialists are new friends that you need to get to know like they are your best friends.
3. When you give a gift to someone, a relationship becomes personal. When a relationship is personal, it can develop into a great friendship.
4. A small gesture of kindness can change a person's mood.

Our Prayer for You

Dear Almighty God, thank you for Your love and creativity. Help us to find creative ways to love others, meeting them in their pain and supporting them through their grief and victories. As we see your creativity in this world and in nature, we pray that we will be reminded of Your control and hand in everything. In Your powerful name. Amen.

Your Key Notes

CHAPTER 10

Strategies

Nancy: "Hey, KT. What are you doing? I am getting my blood drawn and going to see my medical oncologist today."

Kathryn: "I just had my appointment. I asked my oncologist if there was another aromatase inhibitor I could take."

Nancy: "My doctor changed my anti-estrogen medication because I was not tolerating the first one. I'm doing better on the second medication."

Kathryn: "My doctor told me there are several different kinds, and you just have to figure out what works for you."

Kathryn

All I could think about during my radiation treatments was that I wanted to be "normal" again. I wanted a clean bill of health like I had hit the restart button. I wanted to feel like I did before radiation, before cancer, and even before my hysterectomy. I did not have to fear breast cancer right then, and I was confident about my health. I was seeing my oncologist twice a year. I was getting two mammograms and an MRI a year for the first three years to confirm everything was clear. I met with my radiologist, who looked at my scans and confirmed that I was cancer free. Just having her to talk to and make sure I was healing and returning to "normal" was a huge support.

Since I was estrogen positive, the oncologist put me on an aromatase inhibitor, otherwise known as an estrogen blocker. The medicine I was taking was only for women who are in menopause or beyond menopause. Not having any estrogen, I immediately went into full-blown menopause. I thought I had gone through menopause after my hysterectomy about five or so years earlier. I have to admit, I thought I was one of the "lucky ones" who did not experience hot flashes or brain fog. I was so wrong. When I began the estrogen blocker, I had multiple hot flashes an hour, brain fog, fatigue, sore joints, sleepless nights, headaches, dryness everywhere, and weight gain. I am so sorry to share this not so wonderful news. In my mind, I was far from normal. However, day by day, I learned strategies to overcome my symptoms rather than allowing my symptoms to get the best of me. It is a choice and a learning process. What worked for me may or may not work for you. Trial and error, continuing to learn, and communicating with others was the best way for me to deal with what I faced while taking this medication.

Some days, I was weak and did not want to endure how I felt. Resting was the best use of my time on those days. I learned how to give myself grace to hold off the guilt. My body was different, and I needed a new regimen. It needed time to adjust. Since I was not sleeping well, resting was easy.

One day, a new friend called to invite me over to visit. I did not know much about her except that I loved her passion for the Lord. She had just finished seminary because she wanted to learn as much as possible about the Bible and the Lord. I was not a student at all; school was not easy for me. For her to go to school just to learn and not for a degree was amazing to me. I am so grateful for that day of enjoying tea and pecans together because it revealed I was in a new club. I was now in a club of "survivors." She shared with me her cancer story, which was similar to mine. I'll never forget when she asked me what date I could stop taking the estrogen-blocker medicine. I had not even thought about it. She confessed how difficult taking the medicine was for her. Her parting words to me were: "It is not forever, only temporary." Those words rang in my ears all the way home. As long as I held onto those words of hope and encouragement, I could endure the side effects or whatever the next challenge brought.

> *"I consider that our present sufferings are not worth comparing with the glory that will be revealed in us."* —ROMANS 8:18 (NIV)

Taking this type of cancer-fighting medicine can be compared to taking birth control pills that try to control a woman's reproductive cycle. Several forms work for some women, and other forms work for other types of women. We are all different and require different pill formulas. A group of women that I applaud are those who do not want to be on a pill but commit to a discipline of diet and exercise. Yes, that is an option, but knowing my personality and lifestyle, that was not for me.

Just like I had to experience several types of birth control medicine over a period of months and even years, I had to follow this same path with my aromatase inhibitor. I tried three different types of medicine before I found the right one for me. I wish I could tell you how I knew that particular pill worked for me. My answer is simple: I just knew.

Since everyone is made differently, symptoms are different as well. Treating those symptoms are different, too. I apologize for the confusion. However, there are three tasks that everyone needs to commit to before, during, and after having cancer. Those three tasks are eliminating alcoholic beverages, decreasing the amount of sugar in your diet, and moving 150 minutes or more per week. Right now, I have a little voice screaming in my head asking me if I practice what I preach. I will be the first to admit I love sugar. I confess, ice cream is my favorite food, and it is not even "food." I love a great cocktail, but it doesn't like me. The sugar in these items make me feel like I am living inside a body that is over one hundred years old. When my body hurts, walking is the last thing I want to do, but I do it anyway. Changing my mindset is my weapon against these temptations. It is a choice that does not come like switching on and off a light. It takes time, practice, and creating healthy barriers.

"Yesterday is not ours to recover, but tomorrow is ours to win or to lose." —LYNDON B. JOHNSON

For me, taking the estrogen blocker causes pain in my hands. My thumbs often feel broken or, more so, like the ligament has been torn. Most of the time, the pain is in my right hand, but sometimes, it's in my left hand. At times, both hands have felt inflamed and achy. I have never had a broken wrist or finger, but, when my symptoms flare up, the pain sure feels similar. Squeezing out toothpaste, sewing, or picking up a glass of water can be excruciating. I have talked to other cancer survivors who have had hand surgery, but those surgeries did not help as much as they had hoped. Since, in my opinion, surgery is the last option, I have found that injections given by my rheumatologist have helped. I can only have injections every three to four months. When my hands hurt before it is time to receive another injection, I have learned that ice baths, followed by heat, have helped tremendously. I also wear braces that look like gloves that people with arthritis wear, which give my thumbs support and rest. CBD oil or over-the-counter anti-inflammatory creams help as well. Lately, I have discovered my swollen hands respond to ginger, cinnamon, and hot lemon tea. I sometimes have a cup in the afternoon or before bed.

Other treatments and therapies for aches and pains include massages, yoga, acupuncture, and float therapy. Because I had a few lymph nodes removed, I refrain from having a massage on my arm and shoulder on the side of my lumpectomy, which could cause unwanted issues with lymphedema. A warm bath with Epsom salts is a great way to relax as well as remove any tenderness. Whether I take a hot shower or bath, I always stretch my back and neck as soon as I leave the water. Having a pedicure and manicure is a quick way to get a leg or hand massage. Ask the manicurist to rub out the tender areas on your thumbs and backs of your legs.

New research is ongoing with patients who struggle with side effects of cancer medication. I met a doctor in Atlanta who is focusing on this problem. Researching ways to reduce complications from medicine will hopefully help eliminate those complications in the future.

While we are all too familiar with ads of medicine promising life-changing results, the side effects of those drugs, for the most part, may sound utterly horrific. Taking the aromatase inhibitor is like that commercial. I have asked myself over and over again if it is worth it to take this medicine and endure the side effects so I can hope not to hear the words "You have cancer" again.

With the counsel of all of my doctors from Atlanta and Birmingham, I have made the decision to maintain the course and follow the regimen. "It's only temporary!" However, I have also made a commitment to take care of my health by eating properly, exercising regularly, eliminating foods that are harmful, and gaining information about the chemicals in our environment. Making a choice to better yourself is the best direction in this journey.

Nancy

I was extremely relieved and beyond grateful when my cancer treatments were over, and I was so ready to start the next chapter of my life. I desperately wanted to get back to my daily routine and live life again. I wanted to improve my health and decrease my stress, so I needed to rethink my mindset. Mindset plays an important role in your relationship with life. By having positive thoughts, you will be able to focus more on things that matter and not on things that zap your energy.

As I thought about my health, I was determined to restructure my life. I had to ask myself what I could do differently to take better care of myself. As I started taking responsibility for my health, I knew I was my own advocate, and I needed to make some changes. Making changes can be challenging, and it requires making choices. We all can change something to make our lives a little better. First, recognize your strengths and use them.

"I have one life and one chance to make it count for something . . . My faith demands that I do whatever I can, wherever I am, whenever I can, for as long as I can with whatever I have to try to make a difference." —JIMMY CARTER

Worry can cause stress, and both can be hard on our bodies over time.

Worry is not reasonable, helpful, or necessary. Also, worry can zap your energy and lead to despair. But somehow, I continue to worry. My goal is to create a peaceful and calm life, which is very hard to do, right? I have been told that 90 percent of the things we worry about never happen. So, there you go. Let's get to work.

> *"My life has been filled with terrible misfortune; most of which never happened."* —MICHEL DE MONTAIGNE

Unfortunately, one of my biggest obstacles is managing my stress and relaxing. It is hard for me to turn off and relax. My husband says that when we go on vacation, it takes me about three days to sit and relax.

When possible, I take fifteen to thirty minutes a day to sit. I read a book, meditate, or watch something uplifting on television. I put my phone on the counter and unplug. This helps to work on the inner self, which can benefit your overall health.

> *"A heart at peace gives life to the body . . ."*
> —PROVERBS 14:30 (NIV)

I also chose to make some lifestyle changes that I felt were safe and effective for me. My tumor was estrogen positive. I was placed on hormone therapy, such as aromatase inhibitor, which is an estrogen blocker. My doctor told me that aromatase inhibitors lower estrogen levels, which can help lower the risk of breast cancer. The type of medication and length of taking it is different for everyone. I was told I would be on it for five years. Trust me when I say that I count down the months. The side effects of the second medication they put me on are not as bad as the side effects of the first one. I just do not like to take medications, but I do know it's important to decrease the risk of my cancer returning. If you are having any side effects from a medication you are taking, please mention it to your doctor. Maybe you can switch to another one. Hopefully, there will be one that you will be able to tolerate.

I started reading as much as I could and learning new ways to live a healthier lifestyle; it was important for me to work on my outer self. There is a lot of advice and information on the internet. Read and learn what will work best for you. Everyone is different, and it can get complicated.

I was very apprehensive about the products I used in our home. I started evaluating everything from household cleaning products to laundry detergent. I chose to use nontoxic and chemical-free brands. I read and studied about ingredients used in foods. When buying foods, if at all possible, buy organic. It is important to eat a well-balanced healthy diet, including fruits, vegetables, whole grains, fish, grass-fed meats, and beans. Drink eight glasses of water a day to stay hydrated, and it will help you feel less fatigued.

Getting enough quality sleep is essential for our bodies to heal. It improves our mood and health. Exercise also plays a vital role in your health. It is great to change it up and do different types of exercises, including strength training. If you can't do anything else, take a walk. It doesn't have to be a long walk. Just get out and take advantage of nature. Nature is a great way to accept beauty and peace. Inhale, exhale, left foot, right foot, and breathe. Be in harmony with yourself and God. I have to remind myself often that I need to think about how far I have come and not how far I need to go.

> *"Focus on giants—you stumble; focus on God—giants tumble."*
> —MAX LUCADO *(Cast of Characters:*
> *Common People in the Hands of an Uncommon God)*

Another thing to consider is starting your day with prayer, thanking God for a new day. I truly believe your first thoughts of the day are important in pointing your day in the right direction. You can say, "I am grateful and loved. I am going to be kind and patient today. I am going to love more and laugh a lot; therefore, I am going to have a great day."

Key Scripture

ISAIAH 30:21 (NIV)

"Whether you turn to the right or to the left, your ears will hear a voice behind you, saying, 'This is the way; walk in it.'"

Key Lesson

The Bible tells us that we will experience trials and tells us how to respond.

"And the God of all grace, who called you to his eternal glory in Christ, after you have suffered a little while, will himself restore you and make you strong, firm and steadfast." —1 PETER 5:10 (NIV)

Knowing this encourages us to make sure we are ready in mind, body, and spirit.

David, the young shepherd who defeated the great Philistine giant, is a great example of being ready. Recognizing lessons from our past gives us strength to face the giants in our future. While David was merely a young shepherd boy, he had a relationship with his Heavenly Father. While he tended his father's sheep, he spent time worshipping by singing and praying. He drew strength and his faith grew by daily praising and honoring God. In turn, God protected him and equipped him to fight the lions and bears that came to attack him and his sheep.

When David heard about the threatening Philistine giant and the terrible things he was saying about Israel, he offered to fight the enemy himself.

"David said to Saul, 'Let no one lose heart on account of this Philistine; your servant will go and fight him.'

"Saul replied, 'You are not able to go out against this Philistine and fight him; you are only a young man, and he has been a warrior from his youth.'

"But David said to Saul, 'Your servant has been keeping his father's sheep. When a lion or a bear came and carried off a sheep from the flock, I went after it, struck it and rescued the sheep from its mouth. When it turned on me, I seized it by its hair, struck it and killed it. Your servant has killed both the lion and the bear; this uncircumcised Philistine will be like one of them, because he has defied the armies of the living God. The Lord who rescued me from the paw of the lion and the paw of the bear will rescue me from the hand of this Philistine.'

"Saul said to David, 'Go, and the Lord be with you.'

"Then Saul dressed David in his own tunic. He put a coat of armor on him and a bronze helmet on his head. David fastened on his sword over the tunic and tried walking around, because he was not used to them.

"'I cannot go in these,' he said to Saul, 'because I am not used to them.' So he took them off. Then he took his staff in his hand, chose five smooth stones from the stream, put them in the pouch of his shepherd's bag and, with his sling in his hand, approached the Philistine.

"Meanwhile, the Philistine, with his shield bearer in front of him, kept coming closer to David. He looked David over and saw that he was little more than a boy, glowing with health and handsome, and he despised him. He said to David, 'Am I a dog, that you come at me with sticks?' And the Philistine cursed David by his gods. 'Come here,' he said, 'and I'll give your flesh to the birds and the wild animals!'

"David said to the Philistine, 'You come against me with sword and spear and javelin, but I come against you in the name of the Lord Almighty, the God of the armies of Israel, whom you have defied. This day the Lord will deliver you into my hands, and I'll strike you down and cut off your head. This very day I will give the carcasses of the Philistine army to the birds and the wild animals, and the whole world will know that there is a God in Israel. All those gathered here will know that it is not by sword or spear that the Lord saves; for the battle is the Lord's, and he will give all of you into our hands.'

"As the Philistine moved closer to attack him, David ran quickly toward the battle line to meet him. Reaching into his bag and taking out a stone, he slung it and struck the Philistine on the forehead. The stone sank into his forehead, and he fell face down on the ground."
—1 SAMUEL 17:32–49 (NIV)

Just like God equipped David to fight Goliath, I believe He equips us to fight our giants. As we sing and give praise, gain knowledge from God's Word, and join others in fellowship as well as work, we learn what the enemy is and ways to defeat it. Some of our enemies may be subtle, such as pride or self-pity. Other enemies may be addictions or temptations that are sure to destroy our relationships and our lives.

Cancer is an enemy we never wanted to fight. I know that in my own strength, the battle would leave me wounded, scared, and useless. However, with the Lord in my heart and on my side, I will be victorious whether the outcome is or is not exactly how I wanted it to be. Just like David, focusing on God's presence and not my circumstances prevented me from becoming discouraged and giving up.

Someone once asked why David picked up five stones when he trusted God to assist him in fighting Goliath. The phrase "You never know . . ." comes to my mind. In his experience of fighting lions and bears, carrying a pocketful of stones was probably normal. In fighting cancer, choose five verses to put in various places to help fight the battle over negativity or depression in your mind. Arm yourself with God's Word. Remain in His presence. Having cancer is like having a very difficult teacher or professor that no one wants. Yet, through the challenging class, principles and concepts will be learned and tested thoroughly. Faith, trust, courage, hope, and priorities are the lessons learned through breast cancer. When the class is over, celebrate!

—KATHRYN

"Jesus looked at them and said, 'With man this is impossible, but with God all things are possible.'" —MATTHEW 19:26 (NIV)

KEY RECIPE

A mocktail is a cocktail without the liquor. This Mojito is infused with mint, which makes this a refreshing and sophisticated beverage you can drink any time of the day or night.

MOJITO MOCKTAIL

1   tablespoon (or more) coconut sugar
    Leaves of 1 small bunch fresh mint
    Coarse salt and coconut
    sugar to taste
1   lime, cut into wedges
    Juice of 4 limes (about ½ cup)
    Soda water to taste

Muddle the coconut sugar and mint leaves using a mortar and pestle or a small bowl and the end of a rolling pin. Mix equal parts of coarse salt and coconut sugar to taste on a plate. Run a lime wedge around the rim of 2 tall glasses. Dip the glasses in the salt mixture to coat the rim. Place a handful of ice in each of the glasses. Combine the mint mixture and lime juice in a glass and mix well. Divide the mixture between the 2 ice-filled glasses. Add enough soda water to reach the desired taste. Garnish each serving with a sprig of mint. Serves 2.

KEY RECIPE

Also referred to as Haymaker's Punch, this is a simple drink that farmers used to enjoy after working in the fields all day. First introduced in the Colonial era, versions of this beverage can be made using different sugars—from honey to molasses to maple syrup. Other spices such as cinnamon, turmeric, and/or cayenne pepper can be added to spice it up. Ginger Switchel is a simple non-alcoholic beverage that is refreshing for both the mind and the body. Loaded with flavor, it also nourishes, hydrates, and detoxifies. The best part of this liquid concoction is that it can be made to satisfy anyone's taste by using substitutions, adding it to tea or lemonade, or serving it hot. The Ginger Juice can be kept in a covered jar in the refrigerator for up to one week.

....

GINGER SWITCHEL

    ¼   cup Ginger Juice (below)
    1   tablespoon unfiltered apple cider
    1   tablespoon fresh lemon juice
    1   teaspoon to 1 tablespoon honey or maple syrup
        Mineral water or club soda to taste

Mix the Ginger Juice, apple cider, lemon juice and honey in a small bowl. Pour over crushed ice in a tall glass. Add the desired amount of mineral water. Garnish with a sprig of rosemary, a honeycomb cube or a cinnamon stick, or sprinkle with ground cinnamon, turmeric powder or cayenne pepper.

    Note: Liquid Stevia may be added if the honey is not sweet enough.

GINGER JUICE

1   (4-inch) piece of ginger root, peeled and rinsed
2   cups filtered water

Dice the ginger root into small cubes. Combine the ginger cubes and water in a small saucepan. Bring to a boil. Reduce the heat to medium-low. Cook, covered, for 15 minutes. Strain out the ginger root. Chill the ginger juice for several hours or overnight. The juice may be stored in a jar in the refrigerator for up to a week.

Key Takeaways

1. Like David found five stones, find five Bible verses and write them down to remind you that God is with you.

2. It is not a waste of time to educate yourself to prevent and treat adverse reactions to medicines.

3. Exercise is the best way to combat the side effects of taking an estrogen blocker.

4. Allow yourself grace when your body is screaming to rest.

5. Keep a journal of your side effects and how you treat them. Keep your doctor updated.

Our Prayer for You

Dear Father God, we give You thanks for allowing us to come into Your presence through the death of Your Son, Jesus. We acknowledge that You know our battle and have equipped us with tools for the fight, such as knowledge, doctors, friends, family, and Your true and holy Word. We trust this trial will bring glory to You as we desire to grow in our faith and persevere. Amen.

Your Key Notes

Barbara
Lavallet

CHAPTER 11

Overcoming Fear

Kathryn: "Hey, Nance. How are you doing today?"

Nancy: "I'm good. At least that is what I believe."

Kathryn: "I have to believe that, too, for you and me."

Nancy: "With God in control, every day will be good."

Kathryn

Since my diagnosis, I have talked to many women who have joined the breast cancer survivors club. I have learned from those who had cancer before me as well as those who were diagnosed after I was that fear is the biggest hurdle to clear. Not knowing what your future holds is a scary position. Living in faith that our Heavenly Father knows us personally and knows what is best for us brings me immeasurable peace.

> *"I don't know what the future may hold, but I know who holds the future."* —RALPH ABERNATHY

Listening to music is how I get recalibrated when my thinking goes haywire. When I am down, anxious, hurt, or weary, simply turning on Christian music helps me change my negative and fearful thinking to that of hope and peace. When I was in college and did poorly on a test or assignment, I would go back to my dorm room and listen for hours to a singer named Twila Paris. I still do that today even though it has been more than thirty-six years.

DO I TRUST YOU
by Twila Paris
Sometimes my little heart can't understand
What's in Your will, what's in Your plan.
So many times I'm tempted to ask You why,
But I can never forget it for long.
Lord, what You do could not be wrong.
So I believe You, even when I must cry.
Do I trust You, Lord?
Does the river flow?

Do I trust You, Lord?
Does the north wind blow?
You can see my heart,
You can read my mind,
And You got to know
That I would rather die
Than to lose my faith
In the One I love.
Do I trust You, Lord?
Do I trust You?
I know the answers, I've given them all.
But suddenly now, I feel so small.
Shaken down to the cavity in my soul.
I know the doctrine and theology,
But right now they don't mean much to me.
This time there's only one thing I've got to know.
Do I trust You, Lord?
Does the robin sing?
Do I trust You, Lord?
Does it rain in spring?
You can see my heart,
You can read my mind,
And You got to know
That I would rather die
Than to lose my faith
In the One I love.
Do I trust You, Lord?
Do I trust You?

I will trust You, Lord, when I don't know why.
I will trust You, Lord, till the day I die.
I will trust You, Lord, when I'm blind with pain!
You were God before, and You'll never change.
I will trust You.
I will trust You.
I will trust You, Lord
I will trust You.
I will trust You.
I will trust You.
I will trust You
I will trust You.
I will trust You, Lord.

Source: Musixmatch

Songwriter: Twila Paris

"Do I Trust You" lyrics © New Spring Publishing Inc.

Our minister shared a story that many preachers have shared from the pulpit. It has been around for several years so you may have heard it. It goes like this:

There was a man walking along a cliff when he fell off it. It was dark, and he couldn't see below. He grabbed a branch and was hanging around for some time. He cried out to anyone who was up there for help. There was silence for a time, and then a voice said, "Yes, do you want help?"

"Yes! I want help," he replied, thinking what a dumb question. "Who are you?"

"I am God" came back the response from above.

"God?"

"Yes, I am Yahweh, King of Kings and Lord of Lords, God. You know, the one who knows all and who loves everyone, who is holy and who seeks to save the lost."

"But what about the people like me hanging off the cliff? Are you going to help me?"

"Yes! What do you need?"

Another dumb question from the creator of the world, he thought. "I need to get down without hurting myself."

"Then, let go."

"What, let go?"

"Yes, just let go."

The man thought about it for a few minutes and then asked, "Is there anyone else up there?"

—Toast Finder: Short stories for any occasion!; toastfinder.com

When you think about this man's fears, you see that he was desperate and needed rescuing. Yet, he was more scared to trust in God, who he could hear and not see. All God was asking was for the man to let go. That probably sounded so foolish to that man on the cliff. No matter what, trust God even if it sounds foolish. If He's got the whole world in His hands, surely, and I believe, He has each of us, too.

When I am out of control of my circumstances, I feel fear, anxiety, and stress. Yet, I quickly change my perspective to one of trust, faith, and hope. Knowing God knows my yesterdays, today, and tomorrows and that He loves me so much, I am confident of what lies ahead.

We have a little mountain cabin just outside of Fort Payne, Alabama, in a town called Mentone. When I drive on Interstate 59, going back and forth between Birmingham and Mentone, I have to pass many eighteen wheelers.

Those massive trucks traveling at high speeds used to make me cringe with fear when I was passing them. However, I learned a technique to help me pass them safely. When I focus on the yellow line to the left of the road, observing the curve or direction in the line, and follow it, I am safe. If I get distracted by looking in the rearview mirror or side mirrors, or even at the truck itself, I lose perspective and judgment. My heart races, my knuckles whiten, and I have to force my eyes not to shut. Even if I can just see part of the yellow line, I know I am safe. I have learned that if I focus on Christ as my yellow line, sometimes knowing yet other times not knowing what is ahead, I will be safe as well. I trust in Him as I take one step, one piece, bit by bit at a time. Passing trucks and overcoming trials such as breast cancer are hurdles that can be cleared with the help of others and our relationship with Christ. Every time I am on the highway, I am reminded of this advice: Focus on Christ as my yellow line. I will never forget this nugget of a lesson that was taught to me because of my fear.

Years ago, when I was sitting in the backyard reading the mail while rolling the baby stroller back and forth with my foot, I heard what I thought was a bird playing in the ivy behind me. It was not a bird, but two huge copperhead snakes fighting. They were standing up straight, twirling, and wrestling. I hate snakes and having two fighting so close to where I was sitting made me fearful of my entire yard. I was paralyzed with fear! I hated to go outside. I was constantly looking out the windows for more of those terrifying creatures. Realistically, I had two elementary school–aged boys and a baby girl and could not stay inside our house every day. I made the decision to learn as much as possible about snakes and their habitats. I learned that the reason the two snakes were fighting was not what I had expected. They were fighting to win the prize of mating with a third snake that was near them. Yikes! I learned what to do in the event of a snake bite and how to discern between a poisonous snake and a non-poisonous one. I put rakes, hoes, and shovels around my yard, giving myself a tool of protection if needed. Equipping myself with knowledge gave me freedom from fear when I was in the yard. Equipping yourself with knowledge, friends, prayer, and your faith in the Lord will give you freedom from fear of cancer.

I wish I could say I am never fearful when it comes to doctor's appointments, mammograms, or yearly appointments, but to be honest, I get anxious. Now that I have had cancer, I know the cells could be somewhere in my body and could raise their ugly heads again. I was surprised the first time I was diagnosed. I could not believe I was chosen to have this type of cancer. Being diagnosed again would not surprise me, although I sure hope I don't get it again. I think about cancer probably more than I should. When I take my medicine each night or have an unusual pain in my chest, underarm, back, or lower abdomen, my mind goes down the rabbit hole of "What if?" Thinking the worst is fairly common among cancer survivors. I think most cancer treatment centers are aware of this fear as well. My team in Atlanta was very sensitive to my feelings and the feelings of other patients who felt uneasy. They let me know that if I needed an extra test to make sure I was fine, they could arrange it. Most days, when I have little aches, pains, or "What is that?" moments, I try to blame it on the weather or what I ate rather than my past cancer history. Giving another possible reason for the problem is a lot more comforting than worrying when there is probably nothing to worry about in the first place.

The enemy called cancer required me to be equipped with the tools to fight fear and develop a healthy mindset. Arming yourself with knowledge of modern medicine, holistic medicine, or both, plus a healthy diet and lifestyle, can lead to courage. I randomly discovered that when I talk about snakes or cancer, I become more confident in myself to fight the battle and determined to make changes in my habits. The conversations I've had—the relationships between me and others with similar experiences—crushed any fear. More importantly, prayer—conversations with the Lord—helped me conquer fear and replace it with peace and joy.

Nancy

Fear is a part of the human condition. We are all human, and fear of the unknown is going to happen and cause us to worry and be anxious. It is hard not to think of what can happen in the future and what it will be like, especially when you get a cancer diagnosis.

> *"The only thing we have to fear is fear itself."*
> —FRANKLIN D ROOSEVELT

If at all possible, try not to think of the future and cancer. You will have a lot going on, so work on the here and now—I am here now, and I am grateful for today. Remember, you are awesome, and you are here for a reason. Don't answer when fear knocks on the door.

> *"The Lord himself goes before you and will be with you; he will never leave you nor forsake you. Do not be afraid; do not be discouraged."*
> —DEUTERONOMY 31:8 (NIV)

As I said in an earlier chapter, I tend to suppress my anxieties and fears, which I know is not a good thing to do. One of the hardest things for me to do is to stay calm during the storm, even when I know it will pass.

Fear can cause physiological changes in our bodies, and we can each react differently. That is why it is important to relieve deep hidden fears, which can help you transform your outlook on life and, therefore, be healthier for your body. Faith is the opposite of fear. If possible, refocus any negative thoughts to positive thoughts, and place your trust in the Lord.

"When I am afraid, I put my trust in you. In God, whose word I praise—in God I trust and am not afraid. What can mere mortals do to me?" —PSALM 56:3–4 (NIV)

When I have a pain that was not there before, my mind tends to wander, and I think, "Oh, my gosh, I wonder if the cancer has spread." It is very normal to feel that way. I truly wish I didn't think of cancer every time I have a new pain. However, it is a journey, and I, too, am trying to practice what I mentioned above.

Have you ever woken up during the night with your fears feeling more intense than usual? I have, and my heart and mind start racing. At night, we have less distractions, so when we wake up during the night, we might focus more on the fear, which then causes us to imagine the worst-case scenario. I find myself in a vicious cycle, and I have to remind myself again and again that God did not give us a spirit of fear. So, instead of counting sheep, I start counting my many blessings one by one. Then, before I know it, I am fast asleep.

"Peace I leave with you; my peace I give you. I do not give to you as the world gives. Do not let your hearts be troubled and do not be afraid." —JOHN 14:27 (NIV)

Another suggestion for addressing fear and sleeplessness during the night is to do some deep-breathing exercises. This can help you positively concentrate on your body and not the negative thoughts. Or place a notepad on your bedside table, and write down whatever is on your mind. I was told that there is something about the act of writing something on paper that can help decrease rumination and worry. However, if waking up with feelings of fear becomes a pattern, you might want to talk to your doctor.

Finally, I find that prayer—even repetitive prayer—allows me to focus on the Lord and place my trust in Him.

A Prayer for Confronting Fear
Heavenly Father,
When I feel crushed by my own worries,
Lift my mind and help me to see the truth.
When fear grips me tight and I feel I cannot move,
Free my heart and help me to take things one step at a time.
When I can't express the turmoil inside,
Calm me with Your quiet words of love.
I choose to trust in You, each day, each hour,
each moment of my life.
I know deep down that I live in Your grace, forgiven,
restored by Your sacrifice. You have set me free.
Amen. —UNKNOWN

When a good friend of mine found out she had breast cancer, she named her cancer Hector. Before surgery, she told Hector to get the heck out of her body. By inserting humor into her journey, her fear decreased, and it gave her hope that the cancer would be gone and out of her body after surgery.

Another friend reminded me that fear is going to happen. We can't dismiss fear when we have a new pain or anything out of the ordinary. Our human tendency kicks in, and we forget that God is in control. Give yourself grace when you feel fear. Keep praying and communicating with God. Also, choose to navigate your day; it is up to you. Don't give in to fear. Make a conscious decision to get up every morning and prepare yourself for a positive day. My friend has a very great point, and I appreciate her advice.

"Commit to the Lord, whatever you do, and he will establish your plans." —PROVERBS 16:3 (NIV)

Fear is not just a manifestation within us about the cancer. We may struggle with the fear of how it will affect others that are in our lives. Here's a specific example: I had an allergic reaction to my second chemotherapy treatment. My husband was out of town, and I had a dear friend from out to town who stayed with me and took me to my treatment. During the night I ran a high fever, and unfortunately, I was admitted to the hospital. I asked my friend not to let my children know yet because I did not want to alarm them. I also did not want to inconvenience my friend.

We must recognize that it is natural and normal to see fear in others around us. My friend shared that she was afraid for me and feared she had inadvertently done something to exacerbate the situation. Seeing fear in others may lead to the fear of letting someone down. It is important to recognize that fear in others without feeling guilty.

It is very important to recognize our limitations when dealing with others, both personally and professionally. We must also recognize that when we carry our problems and other people's problems, including fear, it is not healthy for us. Do not be afraid of saying "no." We must do what we are comfortable with, but we need to set boundaries and take care of ourselves first. Then, we will be able to experience the joy of not being fearful and overwhelmed.

Key Scripture

ISAIAH 41:10 (NIV)

"So do not fear, for I am with you; do not be dismayed, for I am your God. I will strengthen you and help you; I will uphold you with my righteous right hand."

Key Lesson

During the time that Nancy and I, with the cookbook team, were developing the Junior League cookbook *Tables of Content*, my mother began experiencing strange symptoms. We first thought it was a cold. About a year later, she was diagnosed with Amyotrophic Lateral Sclerosis (ALS), or Lou Gehrig's disease. The disease attacks the neurons from the brain to certain muscles, which will eventually stop working and die. There is no cure or known reason for this disease.

My mother loved to journal and write as she experienced the nearness of the Lord in her life. She wrote a story the day after she was diagnosed with a fatal disease. The depth of her heart and faith is such a great example to all of us, especially to those facing an illness or disease. Rather than sharing a story from God's Word in this chapter, Nancy and I wanted to share this personal story by my mother, Barbara Lavallet.

The Train

It is Thursday morning, June 14th, 2007. I am sitting outside on the deck of a mountain cabin that sits high on the ridge in Mentone, Alabama. The birds are singing, and the sun is shining. I hear a woodpecker and a mockingbird. The winds blow, releasing the rain from the leaves from the night before and sprinkling me as I wait on prayer time. Every day is a new day, a new baptism, promise of a new revelation of God's love. I wait expectantly for a word from my Lord. I ask for a more personal relationship. He is drawing me close.

I have been like the puppy needing a leash lest I go running off to the pleasures and pressures of this world. God has drawn me to Himself with His steadfast hand and now I come and sit at His feet or even in His lap, waiting to be fed and comforted, trusting I will be given love and comfort. He now trusts me with the deeper mysteries of the spiritual world. I wait with anticipation for the secrets to be revealed today.

I must confess there have been many days that I have not had this quiet peace. I would awaken with dread and fear and not want to even face the day. I have been experiencing strange symptoms that cause difficulty when swallowing and speaking. Other symptoms like cramps and pains in my arms and legs would scream that there is something terribly wrong. Anxiety would turn to fear and fear would turn to panic. I would become like the girl in the old silver tone movies that was tied to the train tracks with ropes and the train was coming down the track. All the crying and screaming did not release me. I had no control over my situation. The cords that bound me held firm. The only relief came when I was utterly exhausted and there were no more tears.

This morning in the mountains my spirit is lifted, and I thank the Lord for the day. Far down in the valley I hear a freight train. Even though it is many miles away, I can hear the clack of the wheels and the whistle blow as it nears the crossing in Fort Payne. Finally, I see the train between the trees and watch as it slowly rolls down the valley. Then I hear a voice speak to my heart. It is very forceful and demands attention. "Barbara, the train! The train, Barbara, the train!" I lift my hands and question. "The train…what do you mean?"

"Think, Barbara, think."

Immediately, I see a flashback in my mind of a scene from a silly movie that I had watched with Gracie, my granddaughter, the night before, Night at the Museum with Ben Stiller. He takes a job as a night watchman, but what he doesn't know is the museum characters come to life at night. He experiences many funny and sometimes fearful situations as he encounters the animals and people that have mysteriously come to life.

The one scene that came back to my mind was in the Wild West area of the museum. The tiny wax figures with their angry attitudes reminded me of Gulliver's Travels. They tie up the watchman Lilliputian style with their tiny cords and cause him to fall onto the railroad tracks. The cowboys shout, "Kill him! Throw the switch!" The locomotive starts down the track toward the watchman. He struggles. The train blows the whistle and keeps coming. The music in the movie reaches a loud crescendo. He looks doomed. There is no help in sight. Just as the train is about to roll over him, the watchman turns his head and with his nose knocks the train and it toppled over like the toy that it is. The watchman also realizes at this time that the cords that bind him are only threads which he can easily break. He breaks them and he is free.

As I sit in the cool mountain air, I think about the sweetness of the Lord to give me a simple word picture so I could understand that fear has no substance. I am reminded of the scripture that fear is not from the Lord, but love, and power and a sound mind. He has given me the power to topple a train of fear. Many verses start coming to mind like sweet old songs that I have lodged deep in my memory. From Philippians, I remember,

"Be anxious for nothing." A verse I carried with me through all the hard medical tests can be found in Isaiah 41:13: "For I am the Lord your God who takes hold of your right hand and says to you, 'Do not fear; I will help you.'" In the book of Hebrews, God reminds me, "I will never leave you nor forsake you."

—Barbara Melson Lavallet
(February 4, 1940–July 6, 2008)

"Give thanks to the Lord, for he is good; his love endures forever."
—Psalm 107:1 (NIV)

Although we prayed for a miracle for my mother, God brought her home to be with Him one year later. For that year, however, she heard the train in the distance wherever she was. "Do not fear! Do not fear! Do not fear!" At the funeral, everyone could hear the whistle of the train in the distance. The whistle was the loudest and longest sound I have ever heard. I will never forget my dear high school friend's expression that silently and lovingly expressed to me, "You are going to be fine without your mama. Our God is so great!"

Just like we experienced the day we were born, the day we first went to school, rode a bike, or received our first kiss, we will experience the day we pass away from this earth in death. Just because the diagnosis is cancer, death may or may not be soon. We don't know, but God knows the year, the month, the minute, and the second that we will die. Everyone will die, but everyone also has a choice of location after death. Will you be in the Father's presence in heaven for eternity? He has given us that choice.

—Kathryn

Loaded with antioxidants, this colorful salad is bursting with fresh flavors and wonderful health benefits.

....

CABBAGE SALAD WITH BEETS AND CITRUS DRESSING

3	red beets
1	tablespoon lemon juice
½	head green cabbage, cored and finely shredded
½	head red cabbage, cored and finely shredded
1	large carrot, finely julienned
⅓	cup cilantro leaves, chopped
	Citrus Dressing (at right)

Scrub the beets and cut off the stems. Peel the beets and cut into quarters. Place in a large saucepan. Add enough water to cover the beets. Add the lemon juice. Bring to a boil. Reduce the heat to medium-low. Simmer for 30 minutes or until the beets are tender; drain. Let stand to cool.

Cut the beets into bite-size pieces. Combine the green cabbage, red cabbage, carrot, beets and cilantro in a large bowl. Drizzle the Citrus Dressing over the cabbage mixture and toss to mix well. Adjust the seasonings.

CITRUS DRESSING

3 tablespoons lime juice (about 2 limes)

3 tablespoons orange juice (1 orange)

2 teaspoons pure maple syrup

¼ cup extra-virgin olive oil

1 tablespoon rice vinegar or red wine vinegar

2 garlic cloves, peeled and minced

1 teaspoon salt

½ teaspoon pepper

Whisk the lime juice, orange juice, maple syrup, olive oil, rice vinegar, garlic, salt and pepper in a small bowl.

Key Takeaways

1. Find a song that will help relieve your anxiety and fears.

2. Whenever you hear a train's whistle, remind yourself: "Do not fear, do not fear, do not fear."

3. Sit quietly and await with anticipation what God is going to reveal in you.

Our Prayer for You

Father God, we give thanks that we have nothing to fear when we believe You will hold us with Your righteous right hand. Since You are the creator of the universe, You know everything—every detail and every secret place in our hearts—how can we not put our lives under Your control? May Your name be glorified, and Your will be done in our lives today and forever. In the holy name of Jesus. Amen.

Your Key Notes

Conclusion

The journey of having breast cancer forever changed both of us. While we love talking with friends, friends of friends, and even strangers about our journey, writing our story—sharing our hearts and what we learned together—has been even more significant. Writing our stories not only reminded us of our past but also of God's provisions, protection, and promises in His Word. If you ask either of us about our experience with having cancer, we will say—without a shadow of a doubt—that we are so grateful. We have been changed for the better. Our perspectives about life, trials, and tribulations as well as joys and celebrations have taken on a deeper meaning. The one thread that ties them all together is the word "relationship." Our relationships—with others, our Heavenly Father, and each other—were the key ingredient.

When Jesus was asked what the greatest commandment is, he responded,

". . . 'Love the Lord your God with all your heart and with all your soul and with all your mind.' This is the first and greatest commandment. And the second is like it: 'Love your neighbor as yourself.'"—MATTHEW 22:37–39 (NIV)

It all boils down to relationships with others and a relationship with our Heavenly Father; they are the only things that matter. Relationship is the word that got us through our journey. We never could have faced the tests, procedures, waiting, sleepless nights, good days, and bad days without our friendship with each other, our relationships with our loving family and many friends, and, in some cases, strangers, and most importantly, our faith in the Lord.

Kathryn: Nancy, what is the one thing you have learned through having cancer and sharing your story?

Nancy: I thank God for "my bump in the road" and what I have learned from my challenges. And I thank Him for the blessings I receive every day. Many people think that cancer is a death sentence. Having cancer has given me a new outlook on life and a purpose to help others going through it.

I would like to tell our readers to focus on themselves and their health. Do not delay having an annual mammogram. Although it may not be the best day, it is an important day. It can save your life.

Also, strengthen your relationships with the people around you. Connect with friends and stay in touch with them. Relationships can be a source of comfort. As with anything in life, it takes time and effort, but your friends and family can help you endure life's challenges.

We know there are many books written about cancer. We hope that our strategy in writing this book will give you encouragement, that you will learn something, and that you will know you are not alone and are loved.

Thank you, dearest Kathryn (aka KT to me) for your wisdom, loving spirit, and precious soul. You are my inspiration. Your enthusiasm is contagious. I am convinced that our relationship/friendship has grown stronger. Writing this book with you has been a true joy. I have learned so much, and it has truly taken me out of my comfort zone. KT, you are a beautiful writer, but I am more of a technical writer. I am a private person by nature, but I know that by sharing our story, we may help someone in their breast cancer journey.

"Never shall I forget the days I spent with you. Continue to be my friend, as you will always find me yours."
—LUDWIG VON BEETHOVEN

We all are going to have "bumps in the road." We just have to stay strong and get around them or over them. It is easy to get off course and let negative emotions get in our way. It's not how fast we can get around or over the bump but how we react. Let your thoughts radiate positive thoughts and make room for joy and love in your heart. We learn through our mistakes and difficulties. It is just hard to go through them.

It is absolutely hard to imagine that this is just a few chapters in the book that God has written for me. Having breast cancer was a huge disappointment, but I know there is a lot more to my story.

My friends and family know I love sunsets. The sun going down in the sky is so beautiful, but I am truly grateful for each sunrise because I am here another day. You will have good days and bad days, challenges and setbacks, but with God all things are possible, and He sees the whole picture.

"Not only so, but we also glory in our sufferings, because we know that suffering produces perseverance; perseverance, character; and character, hope."—ROMANS 5:3–4 (NIV)

Schedule time for yourself. I participate in a Bible study by phone with two of my friends from high school. During our last Bible study, we came up with the 4 Ps: Pause, Pray, Peace, and Praise. Pause to pray and receive peace as you praise God. Hopefully, this can help you to be still and let God be God.

Even though we might be apprehensive about our future, a good friend told me:

"I do not need to know the final picture to do what
needs to be done. The future will be revealed."
—THE REV. DR. SUSE E. MCBAY, PH.D.

My favorite verse, which I mentioned in an earlier chapter, that gets me through a lot of my ups and downs is:

"I can do everything through Christ, who gives me strength."
—PHILIPPIANS 4:13 (NLT)

I know I must say this several times a day, even when I am skiing down a mountain or doing something uncomfortable like a mammogram. A dear friend gave me a bracelet, which I never take off, that has this verse engraved on it. I will forever cherish it.

Kathryn and I would like to say, "Be bold, courageous, and confident regardless of how you feel. We both have had a life-changing experience, and we are grateful for our blessings."

And, most of all, thank you to our readers, we truly appreciate you. You are in our thoughts and prayers. Bless you!

"And this is my prayer; that your love may abound more and more
in knowledge and depth of insight, so that you may be able to
discern what is best and may be pure and blameless for the day of
Christ, filled with the fruit of righteousness that comes through Jesus
Christ—to the glory and praise of God."
—PHILIPPIANS 1:9–11 (NIV)

Nancy: Ask and you shall receive. I could go on and on, but it's your turn. KT, how has this experience shaped and changed you?

Kathryn: If you were to ask me if I believe in luck, I would tell you unequivocally "no." I believe all things happen for a purpose and reason. However, some things just happen, like when I won a doll at a craft show when I was about seven years old. I do not believe in bad luck either. I am sure I stepped on a lot of cracks, and I never broke my mother's back. While I could go down a rabbit hole talking about this, let's just start with this: I do not believe having breast cancer had anything to do with luck. Only our Sovereign Lord knows how and why I was chosen to have this in my life's story. I am thankful for each day in my life and give thanks for the days I live, knowing I had cancer and that I might or might not have it again in the future.

> *"Rejoice always, pray continually, give thanks in all circumstances;*
> *for this is God's will for you in Christ Jesus."*
> —1 THESSALONIANS 5:16–18 (NIV)

After receiving a devotion from a sweet friend, I was reminded of the fact that God continuously works, shapes, and creates us to be the people He designed us to be. With my cancer diagnosis, I could see it as a benefit in my personal relationship with Him and how that would affect my relationships with others.

Not very long ago, my husband and I took our three children and our two future daughters-in-law to Europe. One day on our trip, we were in Tuscany in a small village called Volterra. This little town is considered the "alabaster capital of the world." We walked down the cute cobblestone streets and poked our heads in the open doors of the artisans' workshops. The artisans were creating beautiful sculptures out of alabaster. At times, they would knock off large and small chunks of stone, which littered the floor. These chunks served no purpose. They were ugly, rough, and unlovely.

As we walked up the street, we ran into a cute little shop that had baskets full of alabaster hearts in all sizes. I bought a handful of these precious hearts to take back home to my friends. These cute little hearts were probably carved out of those ugly chunks of alabaster that I thought didn't have a purpose.

When I was diagnosed with breast cancer and had to endure surgery and radiation, I thought about that devotion my friend sent me and about my little alabaster heart. If that little chunk of stone could talk, it would probably scream to the artisan, "Ouch! Stop that! That hurts! I don't like this pain! Leave me alone!" I felt the same way. I wanted to scream to the Lord to make it stop: "Remove this cancer!" Yet, the artisan would probably reply to the little stone: "Trust me! I'm not finished with you yet. I have a great purpose for you."

The little stone would probably say, "Okay, I trust you." But after more hammering, chiseling, and sanding, the little rock might cry out again!

"I don't like this pain. I have had enough! Please make it go away!"

"Trust me, little stone. I am holding you in my hands. I know the plans I have for you!"

Just as the chunk of stone could only be made into a heart by enduring the pain, through my cancer and pain, I was willing to be chiseled, hammered, and sanded to give me a heart—a heart for Him and a heart for others.

He is our Father. Art is His work. (He+art= Heart—a heart He has created by working in our lives.)

In His mercy and grace, His love for us shapes us and our purpose, making us beautiful.

When you cut out a heart using paper, you fold the paper in half and cut half of a heart. Both sides are exactly the same size and shape, so it mirrors the other side. That is what we need to do with our heart. It needs to mirror the image of our Father and Lord, who lives in our hearts.

Every morning, I raise my feet in the air and swing them to the side of the bed. As I look at my feet, I speak quietly in my mind:

"This is the day the Lord has made; we will rejoice and be glad in it."
—PSALM 118:24 (NKJV)

I started this routine when my father was in palliative care at the hospital, my mother-in-law was just down the hall in Intensive Care, and my father-in-law was coming in for another blood transfusion due to lung cancer. This was all in one day. It was a very dark time for me as I was overwhelmed and grieving. I did not know who or how to help first. However, I learned the routine of raising my feet in the air and reciting the verse from the book of Psalm. It doesn't matter if my days are good or bad, rough or peaceful, chaotic or in order, I trust the Lord knows it before I do, and I am grateful for each day. Just like the anticipation of opening a gift during the holidays or for my birthday, my mind is ready to receive whatever the day reveals.

If my life is a book and each page is a day, I can only live one word at a time, one line at a time, one page at a time, and one chapter at a time. I cannot skip anything that is written in that page or book. I endure the trials, knowing they are shaping me like the chunk of alabaster was shaped into a precious heart. I also sing and shout for joy when God answers a prayer, passion, or secret desire that I have hidden deep in the corners of my heart. He is who He says He is—the creator of the universe—and He fashioned mankind in His very own image.

A vivid memory I have from my childhood happened when I was sitting in the small group of my fourth grade Sunday School class. The teacher took out a match and let it burn until it burned out. He told us our lives are as quick as the flame that burned on the matchstick. I often think about that picture, questioning if what I have done while living on this earth has been significant. I can't think of anything warmer than loving others or anything as consuming as God's love. Those are the things that really matter.

> *"Why, you do not even know what will happen tomorrow. What is your life? You are a mist that appears for a little while and then vanishes."* —JAMES 4:14 (NIV)

After I look at my feet, ready for what God is willing to reveal to me that day, I prepare a cup of coffee and sit in one of three places in my house to pray and read the Word of God. My relationship with God is vital for living, and time spent with Him is vital for our relationship. My relationship with others is just as important. Calling new or old friends, relatives, and neighbors is one important way to love and encourage each other. Joining a church is an excellent way to grow in your relationships with others and your relationship with the Lord. When fighting cancer, I could rely on those two key factors. I believe that is true for everyone.

I am so grateful for my relationship with Nancy, my sweet and precious friend, who went with me through cancer—side by side, two by two, learning and growing, crying and rejoicing. Although we live in different states, I feel like we are next-door neighbors. Her support and love, knowledge, and wisdom have been a lifesaver for me. Jesus sent His disciples and followers out in pairs of two for a reason. Every day, I discover that Nancy and I had cancer at the same time for a reason as well. While Nancy and I had the privilege of walking this road together, so many other relationships with family and friends provided countless hours of support. With Nancy, my friends, and my family by my side, traveling this road alone was never an option.

"After this the Lord appointed seventy-two others and sent them two by two ahead of him to every town and place where he was about to go. He told them, 'The harvest is plentiful, but the workers are few. Ask the Lord of the harvest, therefore, to send out workers into his harvest field.'" —LUKE 10:1–2 (NIV)

Our purpose in writing this book—sharing our stories—is to help anyone who has cancer or knows someone who has cancer and especially breast cancer. While we love talking to others in the same situation, sharing our journey through these pages, allowing the reader to take notes and journal thoughts and feelings, allows more people to feel supported and not alone. We pray and trust this book will be placed in the hands of the reader in God's perfect time. Thank you for allowing us to share our hearts and stories.

"If you declare with your mouth, 'Jesus is Lord,' and believe in your heart that God raised him from the dead, you will be saved. For it is with your heart that you believe and are justified, and it is with your mouth that you profess your faith and are saved." —ROMANS 10:9–10 (NIV)

The Bible says you can only get to heaven by trusting in God through His Son, Jesus Christ. No one can earn their way into heaven. We all have sinned.

"It is by grace you have been saved, through faith—and this is not from yourselves, it is the gift of God—not by works, so that no one can boast." —EPHESIANS 2:8–9 (NIV)

A Simple Prayer

Dear God, in the Bible, You have promised that if I believe in your Son, Jesus Christ, alone, everything I've done wrong in my life will be forgiven. I want to learn and understand the purpose of my life. I trust and believe you will accept me into Your presence—Your kingdom—for all eternity.

I am asking for your forgiveness. I believe that Jesus died, paying the price by His death for my sins, and that you raised Him back to life. I want to trust Jesus as my Savior and follow Him as Lord from now and forever. Help me to do Your will. Guide my steps, and sustain me along my path. In Jesus' name I pray. Amen.

Your Key Notes

What to Say or Do for a Friend Going Through Breast Cancer

- Be prepared for a conversation about cancer or about anything but cancer. If you are going to visit the friend, schedule a time to meet. Never just show up. Keep the conversation brief and read body clues so you'll know when to leave

- Listen! Don't use the time with your friend to share your life's events. Eye contact is sweet and sincere. Allow the patient to vent her feelings.

- Humor has its place but only if the cancer patient begins the conversation. Don't initiate it.

- All cancer situations are different so try not to compare with others.

- Ask what the cancer patient wants to talk about. Being real and normal is what everyone wishes.

- Empathize with your friend: I am so sorry you are going through this. I can't imagine how you feel. I don't know what to say. How can I help?

- Refrain from saying: "I know how you feel. What do you think you did to cause this? I know someone who died. Have you tried this or that?" Comparing someone else's cancer to the patient's is not helpful. Remember this time is draining, and your friend needs to rest, be quiet, and have some space.

- Offer to help by going to appointments with her, providing meals, taking care of her children or pets, or doing her laundry, chores, etc.

- Offer to take your friend around town for a car ride to run errands or to visit various places for a distraction.

What Gifts to Give Breast Cancer Patients

- Heart-shaped pillow to put under her arm after her surgery
- Journal and pens
- Electric blanket or throw
- Lemon candies
- Moisturizer
- Large insulated beverage tumbler
- Books
- Puzzles
- Cute socks
- Stationery set with stamps
- Tea, honey, lemon, cinnamon
- Ginger candy
- Robe
- List of good movies and books
- Back scratcher
- Lip balm
- Really good soft tissues
- Flowers

If she is going through chemotherapy:

- Fun hats
- Soft head scarves
- Herbal neck and shoulder wrap for warming
- Eye mask

About the Cover

Artist Katie Garrison painted the scene in Telluride, Colorado, shown on the cover. Katie lives in Colorado Springs with her husband and two children. Her love of beautiful landscapes continues to be a source of inspiration for her impressionist artwork.

Our conversations about our cancers began over the phone, but the idea of sharing our stories began while we were hiking the trails in Telluride. Along those trails, we walked, talked, and prayed, and the concept of this book came to life. Our desire was to share a simple but important concept: two of the things in life that matter the most are our relationships with others and our relationship with our Heavenly Father.

We will all experience mountains and valleys, highs and lows, sunny days and storms, sunrises and sunsets, and beginnings and endings. God designed the perfect place and reason for each of these moments in our lives, and He will reveal them in His perfect time. Order is in everything He created. The cover art depicts our journey from the valley to the mountain. The road stands for our journey with Christ; He is our connection to God.

The mountains represent special times for both of us—times when we were being still with the Lord. In the mountains, we find refuge from the busyness and demands of life. Seeing the blue sky on the mountain reminds us that, because of our faith, we are in His presence. The valley is where we fulfill His purpose and calling. We rely on His daily protection and guidance and believe He is protecting us against evil all the days of our lives.

Like the mountains, the ocean reflects this orderly rhythmic pattern of highs and lows; however, the motion is constant. A wave cannot be at its peak forever. It must keep moving. The continual movement mirrors our trials—the difficult days in the storms. Like a wave, the difficult situation will eventually end.

Every God-given breath you take follows this calculated and perfect order, like the rise of a mountain, the depth of a valley, and the crest and trough of a wave. You breathe in, and your chest rises. You breathe out, and your chest falls. With every breath, we want to share the love of the Lord with others, shouting it from the mountaintop. Being diagnosed with breast cancer was not in our plans, but it was for His purpose. By sharing the story of how we rode the wave of adversity—how we navigated breast cancer—we hope to encourage you and inspire you to make every breath count.

—KATHRYN & NANCY

About the Authors

Kathryn Tortorici

Kathryn Tortorici lives in Birmingham, Alabama, with Sam, her high-school sweetheart and husband of thirty-five years. She has an Education degree from Auburn University and taught kindergarten for five years. She is blessed with three adult children, two daughters-in-law, and two granddaughters. Kathryn enjoys painting, sewing, and writing. When she is not traveling or involved with Bible study, she is walking her golden retriever. Kathryn's passion is hospitality, serving others in her home, in the community, or in Mentone, Alabama. She loves people and sharing her faith.

Nancy Bynon

Nancy Bynon grew up in Dothan, Alabama. After graduating from Auburn University with a Nursing degree, she moved to Birmingham, Alabama, and worked at the University of Alabama at Birmingham (UAB) Hospital for eight years. UAB is where she met Steve, her husband of thirty-seven years. They have a son and a daughter, a son-in-law, and a precious granddaughter. Pearl, Nancy's loving Labrador  companion, is always by her side. Nancy's favorite leisure activities are spending time with friends and family in Colorado, needlepointing, traveling, and baking.

Kathryn and Nancy were diagnosed with breast cancer in January 2019.

Your Key Notes